Faith, Interrupted

FAITH, INTERRUPTED

A Spiritual Journey

ERIC LAX

ALFRED A. KNOPF · NEW YORK · 2010

This Is a Borzoi Book Published by Alfred A. Knopf

Copyright © 2010 by Eric Lax

All rights reserved. Published in the United States by
Alfred A. Knopf, a division of Random House, Inc.,
New York, and in Canada by Random House of
Canada Limited, Toronto.

www.aaknopf.com

Knopf, Borzoi Books, and the colophon are registered
trademarks of Random House, Inc.

A portion of chapter 7 appeared in somewhat
different form in The Atlantic Monthly as
"The Death of My Father" (July 1978).

Library of Congress Cataloging-in-Publication Data
Lax, Eric.
Faith, interrupted : a spiritual journey /
Eric Lax.—1st ed.
p.   cm.
ISBN 978-0-307-27091-7 (alk. paper)
1. Lax, Eric. 2. Packard, George.
3. Episcopalians—Biography. I. Title.
BX5995.L355A3   2010
283.092—dc22
[B]   2009031503

Manufactured in the United States of America

First Edition

Life is doubt.
And faith without doubt is nothing but death.
—MIGUEL DE UNAMUNO, "Salmo II"

Ah! what a divine religion might he found out
if charity were really made the principle of it
instead of faith.

—PERCY BYSSHE SHELLEY to Leigh Hunt,
as the organ played in the cathedral in Pisa (1822)

Faith, Interrupted

One

St. Alban's Church, 1952

An Episcopal priest is celebrating Holy Communion for seventeen congregants settled in the dark-stained oak pews in a small wood-and-stucco church in a tiny Southern California town in 1953. The prayer he is reading is for the whole state of Christ's Church. It begins, "Almighty and everliving God, who by thy holy Apostle has taught us to make prayers, and supplications, and to give thanks for all men. . . ." He is about ten minutes into a service that began at 7:30 a.m. and will be over by 8:00. This is the quietest and sparest of the three weekly Sunday services: no hymns, no music, no sermon. There are only the lyrical words written in 1545 for the reformed Church of England by the poetic and Machiavellian theologian Thomas Cranmer. This is the same Thomas Cranmer who in 1529 wrote the thesis supporting King Henry VIII's claim that his marriage to Catherine of Aragon was invalid; who for his efforts was made archbishop of Canterbury; who aided Henry in invalidating his second, fourth, and fifth marriages; and the same Thomas Cranmer who, when Protestantism was not kindly looked upon following Britain's return to Catholicism with the coronation of Henry's daughter Mary I in 1553, was burned at the stake as a heretic. (He received the courtesy given to those of a certain rank of being garroted just before the fire was lighted, but in the event, all breath was not wrung out of him, and thus he suffered every agony of both the wire and the flame.)

Neither Cranmer's beautiful language nor his grisly death is on the mind of the eight-year-old acolyte kneeling on the altar step in his red cassock and white cotta (rather like a large linen T-shirt worn over the cassock), a silver cross on a red ribbon around his neck that he received after his first year as an acolyte; there is a silver bar engraved "1953" between the cross and the ribbon, to commemorate an additional year of service. Every Sunday the boy is there to assist the priest at this service, and every Sunday for three or four weeks now he has mysteriously become vertiginous at this very point. As the prayer continues, he will wobble to his feet, his face pasty white and clammy, slip out of the church through the tiny sacristy appended to the priest's office, and double over the four-by-four wooden railing on the small cement porch just in time to vomit onto the rosebush below it. In a few moments his stomach will settle, the color will return to his cheeks, and by the time the prayer ends he will be back on his knees, ready to join the congregation in reciting the General Confession: "Almighty God, father of our Lord Jesus Christ, Maker of all things, Judge of all men; We acknowledge and bewail our manifold sins and wickedness. . . ." (His parents, who are at the service and who believe, though not to extremes, that one should follow the ancient tradition of fasting after midnight before Communion so that the sacred food at the Lord's supper is not touched by worldly fare, soon find that soda crackers and a glass of orange juice before leaving home prevent further attacks.)

The boy quickly refocuses on his duties. He has already moved the red leather-bound missal that contains the order of the service from the right-hand, or Epistle, side of the altar following the reading of the Epistle (a selection from one of St. Paul's letters, or from the Acts of the Apostles or Revelations) to the left, or Gospel, side for the reading of the Gospel (the congregation stands for the Gospel as an acknowledgment of the time in the early Church when there were no pews); brought the priest the ciborium, the sterling silver box of inch-round Communion wafers to place on the paten, a silver plate on which there is a three-inch-round Host, which the priest will raise above his head and break during the Prayer of Consecration in recognition of Christ's broken body on the cross; and, after a quick count of the parishioners in the dozen pews, quietly whispered, "Seventeen." When blessed during the service, the wafers become symbolic of Christ's body, meant to be dissolved on the tongue, rather than chewed. He also has held out the cruets of water and wine for the priest to measure into the chalice, and poured water over the priest's fingertips and into the silver lavabo bowl so that any crumbs of the Sacrament are caught.

As he does every Saturday night before going to sleep, last night the boy knelt beside his bed and read the same two of the 250 pages in *The Practice of Religion,* the three-by-five-inch book given him at his confirmation by his parents and signed by the bishop. He is expected to say in his mind the eight short Acts of Faith, Love and Repentance and the Anima Christi: An Act of Devotion to Jesus in the Blessed Sacrament ("Soul of Christ, sanctify me / Body of Christ, save me / Blood of Christ, refresh me. . . .") that goes on for half a page, which he does unhesitatingly and without thought as to why, as an accepted part of his evening to prepare him for Communion.

He is not thinking of those prayers now. The holiest time of the service approaches, the Prayer of Consecration: "For in the night in which he was betrayed, he took Bread; and when he had given thanks he brake it, and gave it to his disciples, saying, Take, eat, this is my Body, which is given for you. . . ." To honor the moment, the boy folds his body down in obeisance to God, so that his buttocks are on his heels and his head rests on his hands on the altar step. He has had trouble concentrating on the words of late, his thoughts running to baseball and other distractions. He wonders if somehow the Devil is testing him, and he tells himself to concentrate harder this time, not to miss this sacred moment, but these very thoughts become a new distraction, and when he hears "Wherefore, O Lord and heavenly Father," the start of the second part of the prayer, he realizes with annoyance and disappointment that time has jumped and once again his mind has wandered.

The remainder of the service passes quickly: The Lord's Prayer, followed by the Prayer of Humble Access: "We do not presume to come to this thy Table, O merciful Lord, trusting in our own righteousness, but in thy manifold and great mercies. . . ." The priest gives Communion to the boy, who then places a narrow cushion on the floor in the gap in the communion rail that he and the priest entered through and that divides the sanctuary (the area around the altar, where the priest conducts the service) from the choir stalls and the nave (where the congregation sits), and then pulls the sliding rail shut; the cushions that run along the rail provide comfortable kneeling for the communicants, as many as seven at a time. The boy kneels to the side of the altar so that he does not trip the priest as he administers Communion to the seventeen faithful. The priest then consumes the few wafers and little wine that remain so that they are not defiled by being thrown away, and the boy splashes water from the cruet onto the paten and into the chalice to gather up any remaining bits of the consecrated Element. The priest drinks the water with one backward toss of his head and then wipes the chalice with a fair linen cloth.

The priest recites the Prayer of Thanksgiving—"Almighty and everliving God, we most heartily thank thee, for that thou didst vouchsafe to feed us who have duly received these holy mysteries, with the spiritual food of the most precious Body and Blood of thy Son our Savior Jesus Christ. . . ." Then the priest, as he does every Sunday, reads as an extra selection of Scripture the Gospel for Christmas Day, the first fourteen verses of the first chapter of John: "In the beginning was the Word and the Word was with God, and the Word was God. The same was in the beginning with God. All things were made by him; and without him was not any thing made that was made. In him was life; and the life was the light of men. And the light shineth in darkness; and the darkness comprehended it not. . . . And the Word was made flesh, and dwelt among us, (and we beheld his glory, the glory as of the only begotten of the Father,) full of grace and truth." As one, the priest and congregation say "Thanks be to God," and the priest closes the missal.

All is quiet as the priest and boy exit the sanctuary and go into the sacristy. The boy returns with a bell-shaped damper to put out the altar candles. When the last flame is turned to a curl of smoke, the congregation takes that as a sign of dismissal and rises to leave. The priest, who has used this minute to hurry from the sacristy and go down the cement walk by the side of the church, next to the dusty unpaved parking lot, is there to greet them at the church doors as they file out.

By 8:15 the priest, the boy, and the church treasurer are back in the office, emptying the pledge envelopes and counting the loose offering. The treasurer, an accountant on weekdays, notes the amount in the pledge envelopes in his black ledger, which holds the details of the parish's finances. Working crisply but carefully, he uses a retractable pencil to make neat columns and notations, then closes the ledger and puts it in his carrying case. Few words are exchanged as the money is sorted. When the job is done, the conversation picks up as the priest takes the loose offering, five or ten dollars at most, and adds it to the small amount he keeps in a black metal cash box in a drawer of his desk as the discretionary fund most priests have to help a parishioner or a stranger down on his luck.

They walk out of the office and stand for a moment beside the church. It is a relatively long rectangle with a low peaked roof, perhaps two thousand square feet in all. Half is the parish hall, half the church. The property is one arc of a circle separated by six streets that intersect it at equal points. In the center of the circle is the Presbyterian church, larger and older, the biggest in this town of five thousand people. Its landscaping is more mature than its newer neighbor, the eucalyptus trees that edge the property tall and densely leafy. The high bushy cedars along the building's walls are a counterpoint to the sparse vegetation around the Episcopalians', evidence that it is established and well-rooted, while its neighbor is still settling in.

The congregation has gone home by now and the only car by the church is the treasurer's. He drives off after good-byes are exchanged, leaving the priest and the boy. The rectory, finished just months before, is next to the church, down one of the streets that are like spokes to the hub of the circle and across from a vacant lot with high, scraggly weeds. The priest and the boy turn to walk the twenty-five yards to the rectory, for they are father and son.

The boy is an only child. As he and his father enter the one-story house, the smell of frying bacon greets him. His mother, who hurried home to make breakfast after chatting with the parishioners, soon has rashers crisped, and she brings them out with runny-yolk eggs basted with bacon fat and accompanied by slices of homemade bread. Grace is said by the priest, always the same succinct one: "For these and all His mercies may God's holy name be praised. Amen." The three dig in without much conversation because there is less than half an hour to eat and get ready to leave the house again. The family service, with organ and choir and enough people this time to pack the nave, begins at 9:15, and each of the three has a role to play.

The boy's mother, the most devout member of the family, is head of the altar guild. The day before, she and one or two other women arranged flowers for the altar and set up the eucharistic vessels. A gracious companion to her husband, she is always by the church door before and after services to greet the congregants. She invariably sits in a pew about two-thirds of the way back, and her clear soprano helps lead the singing of the hymns. The priest will preach a sermon he thought over during the week and

Faith, Interrupted

wrote the day before. It may be on that Sunday's Gospel but usually is on a more generic topic; either way, it will be conversational in style and instructive of Christian teaching and will last about ten minutes. The boy, having quickly read the comics in the Sunday paper, will once again be an acolyte, joined this time by a second one. The boy does not find this double duty strange; Sunday is his father's busiest workday, and it is as if he is with him in his office.

In the sacristy, the boy and his fellow acolyte, one of his best friends, joke while slipping on their cassocks, cottas, and crosses. The priest deftly puts on his layers of sacred garb: a white linen alb; a green stole, the color of the ecclesiastical season purple for Advent and Lent; white for Christmas, Epiphany, Easter, and Trinity, green for the twenty-four Sundays after Trinity and the twelve after Epiphany; black for Holy Saturday; red for Pentecost, All Saints' Day, and the feasts of the martyrs—held in place around the waist by a cincture, a ropelike length of woven cotton; an oval silk chasuble the color of the stole, elaborately decorated and embroidered with a cross, the Greek letters *chi* and *rho* (for *Christus Rex,* Christ the King) interwoven; and a maniple, a long, narrow strip of the same color and material as the chasuble and stole, draped over his lower left arm and attached to the alb with a metal snap. Originally meant as an ornamental handkerchief, by the Middle Ages it came to suggest the bonds that held Jesus' hands and to symbolize the sorrows of earthly life.

This Sunday the boy is the crucifer, as he often is, holding the seven-foot wooden pole with a bronze cross atop it to lead the procession of the choir, followed by the priest, into the church as the first hymn is sung. He has already partaken of the Sacrament at the early service, and so when it is time to count the congregation, he will not include himself among those who will take it at this one. Where the 7:30 service was quiet and contemplative, this one punctuates the sacred silence with music all can sing. The opening hymn is always something familiar to the congregation—"Glorious Things of Thee Are Spoken, (Zion City of Our God)," "Onward, Christian Soldiers," "Immortal, Invisible (God Only Wise)"—one that can be easily and lustily sung, if often in each person's own key.

The boy attends to his duties, confident that he will not forget to do something or that he will do anything out of order or at the wrong time. This is a ballet he knows step by step, and he hits every cue. He knows it so well, in fact, that the first Saturday of every month his mother unsympathetically rousts the boy out of bed at what is to him the ungodly hour of 9:00 a.m. ("You're turning day into night!") so that his father can use him to go through the motions of the service as a way to train new acolytes and keep old ones in practice; he affectionately calls the boy his "stooge." The boy is unaware that people in the congregation are watching him and his father with pious admiration, but he is not unaware of them. He is adept in quickly counting their number (and in later years checking to see if a particular girl he likes is there), but they are simply part of the pageant. He knows every word of the liturgy and is completely at ease. God's house might just as well be his living room. Sometimes on a weekday when he is in

the church on an errand or to see his father, whose office
is to one side of the chancel, he will come in through the
sacristy on the other side, open the round tin contain-
ers in which the unconsecrated Communion wafers and
priest's Hosts are kept, and help himself. They are slightly
crunchy, paper-thin circles of unleavened flour—the
WASP version of matzo, an item that will not cross the
boy's palate for many years yet—and as they are unconsecrated, there is no sin in snacking on them. He finds the
dryness and slight flavor of the wafers an interesting sensa-
tion, and from time to time he grabs a dozen or so, or a
couple of Hosts, pops them in his mouth, and chomps
with guiltless gusto.

The boy is as comfortable in his faith, as accepting of
God and the Holy Trinity, as are his parents. He knows his
catechism and can rattle off that the word *sacrament* means
"an outward and visible sign of an inward and spiritual
grace given unto us; ordained by Christ himself, as a
means whereby we receive the same, and a pledge to
assure us thereof." The boy knows there are two sacraments generally necessary to salvation, baptism and the
Supper of the Lord, and that there are two parts to each
sacrament: the outward and visible sign, which is baptism
with water in the Name of the Father, and of the Son, and
of the Holy Ghost; and the inward and spiritual grace,
which is a death unto sin, a new birth into righteousness,
and a transformation into a child of grace.

He knows this, but he gives his knowledge no thought.
He knows it in his heart; only the words are in his head. He
accepts it willingly and without reflection or examination.

He gives no consideration to what a sacrament may be beyond the words he knows, or what grace is, or what is the meaning of salvation, or what the words said in the Eucharist of the body and blood of Christ signify. Nor does he think to consider anything about the Trinity, except that God is God; Christ is God's son; the Holy Ghost is God consubstantial with the Father and the Son.

When about a third of the way into the service everyone stands to recite the Nicene Creed, the boy says without pausing to remember what comes next that he believes "in one God the Father Almighty, Maker of heaven and earth, And of all things visible and invisible: And in one Lord Jesus Christ, the only-begotten Son of God; Begotten of his father before all worlds, God of God, Light of Light, Very God of very God; Begotten, not made; Being of one substance with the Father; By whom all things were made: Who for us men and our salvation came down from heaven, And was incarnate by the Holy Ghost of the Virgin Mary, And was made man: And was crucified also for us under Pontius Pilate; He suffered and was buried: And the third day he rose again according to the Scriptures; And ascended into heaven, And sitteth on the right hand of the Father: And he shall come again to judge both the quick and the dead; Whose kingdom shall have no end."

The boy adds that he believes in "the Holy Ghost, The Lord, and Giver of Life, Who proceedeth from the Father and the Son; Who with the Father and Son together is worshipped and glorified; Who spake by the prophets." He believes "in one Catholic and Apostolic Church," and acknowledges "one Baptism for the remission of sins." He looks "for the Resurrection of the dead: And the Life of the world to come."

He adds his "Amen" with vigor. He has stated his belief, accepting as fact, without logical proof or material evidence, what can only be imagined. He has repeated words he has heard since he was an infant. These words, which he says so easily and without examination, are not so much his belief as they are his declaration of faith, faith that requires no evidence to validate, but simply comes from God, a gift to the willing to accept; but even that is a clearer definition than the boy has or needs. He simply has faith. When he is ten, he visits the Grand Canyon with his parents during a car trip across the continent. He slips down a steep incline and, perhaps in fact but certainly in his mind, is headed over the edge and into the abyss when he catches on a bush and his slide is stopped. He assumes that God has saved him, and for many years he carries a certainty of their personal relationship.

He feels God's presence not only in church but also in nature. His father and another priest with a shared interest in young people and their spiritual health find the land for and lead in the opening of a camp in the mountains an hour away. First army-surplus tents are pitched among the Coulter pine and black oak. Soon open-sided A-frame cabins are built. The boy spends part of every summer at the camp until he is in his twenties, and, like the church, it will become a second home. Each night there is a campfire. At one, an astronomer from the nearby Palomar Observatory comes to talk. He points out the Big and Little Dippers, Orion, the Pleiades, Venus, and Mars and then quotes from Psalm 19: "The heavens declare the glory of God; / and the firmament showeth his handy-work." *Of course!* the boy thinks to himself. *Of course!* Decades later, he still will recall those words nearly every time he looks into the night sky.

When the boy is twelve, a new, much larger church is finished on what was the dirt parking lot for the old church, much of the labor done by the fast-growing congregation. His father puts an empty beer can into the trench for the foundation before it is poured to acknowledge all the sweat that poured from the volunteers as they dug it and that will continue to flow in the nearly two years of construction that follow. He doesn't put in a full can, he tells the boy and others with a sly smile and a glint in his eye, because "the good Lord would object to the waste."

On many Saturday afternoons the boy is the acolyte as his father marries a couple, often not long out of high school. He watches with combined amusement and concern as the groom and best man pace nervously in the sacristy before the service. Often, the groom's hands are so swollen from sweat and anxiety that the ring must be forcibly pushed onto his finger by a bride whose own ring seems always to glide on. By the time he is ten, he knows the marriage service word for word, and also believes— and argues with his friends—that all offspring in their (or anyone's) marriage will come not as the consequence of any act between them but as a result of this prayer: "O Almighty God, Creator of mankind, who only art the well-spring of life; Bestow upon these thy servants, if it be thy will, the gift and heritage of children. . . ." One day he will be amazed to discover how the newlyweds might affect matters.

The boy is happy to give up a portion of his free day, not only because he enjoys being with his father but because his father gives him 10 percent of his gratuity from the grateful couple. This being a poor town and it being the 1950s, that gratuity is generally ten dollars, but at a time when the boy's allowance is under a dollar a week, he is happy for the chance to more than double his spending money.

The church, empty virtually all the week except for a morning service on Wednesday and weddings on Saturday, is an occasional lure to the boy. For some years he climbs the stairs to the choir loft at the rear of the nave and makes feeble attempts to learn to play the organ. The usually discordant notes echo and are an immediate rebuke to his lack of practice and discipline; if he *really* wanted to learn, he knows, he would ask for lessons and play daily, but he doesn't.

The silver bars above his acolyte's cross on a red ribbon, each engraved with the year of service, will grow to twelve. With the exception of which girl the boy looks for in the congregation, the Saturdays and Sundays pass almost unaltered, as they did for years before and will continue to do until he leaves California in 1962 to go east to a college affiliated with the Episcopal Church, taking his faith intact. There is a requirement that students attend chapel on campus or services at other churches or a nearby synagogue once a week. The boy goes more often than that, as well as going to the synagogue with friends sometimes. During his first service at the synagogue, he is astonished to discover how similar much of the Hebrew liturgy is to the Episcopal service. After several visits, his friends joke that at heart he really is Jewish. At first he is puzzled by this assumption, but soon he comes to delight in his apparent polydenominational ability. Still, he attends chapel so regularly that when one weekday afternoon the chaplain is called away, he asks the boy to lead evensong, which he does with comfort and pleasure, saying prayers he has known by heart virtually all his life. Afterward a fellow student, whose presence is due to mandate and not choice, admiringly tells him, "You have balls." The boy smiles and shrugs, having done only what comes naturally.

In the current, modern-English Episcopal liturgy the priest says just before the congregation comes forward for Communion, "Therefore we proclaim the mystery of faith," to which he and the congregation join in saying, "Christ has died. Christ is risen. Christ will come again." As the boy grows older, he often contemplates the mystery of faith, and he finds that as he ages, the faith of his childhood is its own mystery.

Two

I, of course, was that boy.

For all my childhood, it was as if faith were part of my DNA, determining but unseen. There was a good reason. When my father was ten, he stepped into a long line of family church-bell ringers, active churchgoers. His name—John Martin Lax—is in the parish register in Swallownest, Yorkshire, England, where he was born in 1904. The name of his father, Luke Martin Lax, is also there, as are the names of preceding generations of Martin Laxes (my grandfather was known by his middle name) who joined others below the belfry of the red church and pulled the ropes in ordered sequence to peal the sounds of Sunday. (One of my middle names is Martin, as is one of my elder son's; the younger is named John.) When my father—always called Jack, rather than John—was twelve,

Martin and his wife, Annie, a former schoolteacher, moved their family of six children, Jack the youngest, a few miles north, into a small two-story stone house in the coal-mining village of Elsecar, where he became under foreman of the colliery.

Martin was a stout man with a bushy mustache, and every night as the radio broadcast Big Ben's first peal of 9:oo p.m. in London, he walked out of the house and then went with a friend to the local pub, where he had a single half-pint of beer; he returned home on the first peal of 1o:oo. He had specific ideas for his sons' futures. For my father, one aspect was that he would have nothing to do with mining, perhaps in part because shortly after moving to Elsecar, my father went to visit Martin at the mine and had his left hand in the wrong place when a piece of machinery was turned on, thereby severing the middle two fingers at the second knuckle. (He dealt with the disfigurement with humor. A joke of his was to hold up the hand as if ordering in a noisy bar and say, "Three beers.") For whatever reason, Martin was determined that his youngest son would be a draftsman, someone who would draw accurate representations of objects for engineering and architectural needs. An apprenticeship with a firm in Sheffield was arranged, and for several years my father dutifully, though increasingly unhappily, followed his father's wishes. But his heart (at least that part not given to his fiancée, a local girl named Enid), and especially his soul, lay in the Church, whose teachings rooted deeply in him, as they did in his father and his siblings: One of his brothers was people's warden; a sister was the parish secretary. In Elsecar, my father combined bell ringing with helping in the services at Holy Trinity, the parish church, a short walk away, and in his early twenties, he gave up his weekend runs with friends through the local fields and on the nearby dales to spend the days with an Anglican order of monks in nearby Mirfield. Mirfield's Community of the Resurrection, founded in Oxford in 1892 and moved from the realm of ideas and talk "to where the industry is" (as they put it) in 1898, is still going today. It is, and was then, based on the Rule of Saint Benedict, so the order has one foot in the community and the other within its walls; brothers go to preach and teach, while the monastery welcomes people for short retreats. My father was regularly among those who went to Mirfield for prayer and introspection, and after a year or so of these visits to test his sense of vocation, he was convinced that he had a calling from God to do His work.

That someone has a calling, that a person in prayer has heard or felt God moving him or her toward a priestly vocation, was not only accepted in our household as I grew up; it was demanded for entering the ministry and an expected part of making big decisions, though it was not expected that the deity would immediately weigh in every time an opinion was sought. The calling my father and his colleagues received and valued was personal and exclusive. Their mission was to take the word of God to others, but not to deliver it with violence of any kind. The "inward and spiritual grace" mentioned in the catechism can also be thought of as an inward and spiritual feeling— the quiet connection with the Almighty. It was to that feeling you turned and listened and hoped to hear an answer.

To listen in prayer was the trick. Both my father and my

mother had learned to present themselves and then be silent, and they lived their lives with what they believed to be a rich intimacy with God through Jesus Christ. They tried to instill that same ability in me, and I followed without a thought. I said my prayers morning and night as I knelt beside my bed. In church I was quick to kneel after I took a pew before the service, then engaged in a prayerful warm-up of letting God know I was there, and I said a prayer of farewell in the time before the acolyte put the damper over the candles to signal the end of the service. At the time, I thought myself devout and in communion with God. It was all very simple, in part because I was a kid and had insufficient experience with life to see the larger implications of faith, and also because my faith had never been tested. My praying, which I did regularly into my thirties, was a one-sided conversation, with me the one yapping on. I seldom asked for anything, and if I did, it was prefaced by the submissive and somewhat oleaginous "If it is your will." In general, I figured there was no point in requesting something from God. Having been an acolyte at so many services—Holy Communion, Morning Prayer, Evening Prayer, the Solemnization of Matrimony—for so many years, I knew the words to them all cold, and as far as I was concerned, the opening sentence of the opening prayer of the service of Holy Communion, the one I attended most of all, made the situation perfectly clear: "Almighty God, unto whom all hearts are open, all desires known, and from whom no secrets are hid. . . ." If God knew everything I wanted, not to mention all my feelings and intimate privacies, there wasn't much point in stating the obvious. So my prayers were either rote recitations or supplications in which I said, "You already know," and involved very little listening. Recently, in an effort to reconnect as part of the work on this reflection, I discovered that it is unsettling trying to pray without words. Speaking to God is easy. Listening for what He might have to tell you requires practice and the spiritual version of athletic training; you have to be in proper shape to function in a different language and dimension than everyday talking.

My father, however, listened, and one answer came in a human voice. In 1927, when he was twenty-three, he heard the Right Reverend Malcolm Taylor McAdam Harding, bishop of the Anglican Diocese of Qu'Appelle in Saskatchewan, in what in the recent past had been the Northwest Territories of Canada. The bishop had come to England on a combination vacation and hunting trip for financial support for his mission work and to find new priests. He wanted clergy with parochial experience in England, rather than new graduates out of Oxbridge or diocesan theological colleges. But even more than already ordained, experienced priests, the bishop was looking for young men of faith to go to this frontier of European settlement to attend seminary at St. Chad's College in Regina so they would have firsthand experience of the prairie and the working conditions they would encounter as priests. Bishop Harding encountered no shortage of candidates. A white-bearded man with apparently a compelling speaking manner, he galvanized my father with his pitch to join him in tending to the spiritual care of the farmers and small businessmen who were settling the massive area, as well as to that of the remnants of the Blackfoot, Cree, Sioux, and more than a half dozen other nations who had been forced by the government to give up their lands at the end of the nineteenth century and now were stowed on reservations, many of which had Anglican schools.

My father was vetted by the bishop and the Qu'Appelle Association in England and invited to go to Canada. In September 1929, he bade good-bye to Enid, to his parents, to his brothers, his sisters, his nieces, and a nephew. Despite Bishop Harding's efforts to enlist men who would stay on the prairie, everyone (with the probable exception of my father) in Elsecar believed he would return after seminary. (When it did become clear that he was not going to return, Enid—probably encouraged by her parents— refused his proposal that she come to Canada and the unknown, and the romance ended. She later married a priest in England.)

On the boat with my father were three of the six other aspirants netted by Bishop Harding. They sailed from Liverpool to Montreal, then went on by train to Regina, a trip of nine days. Classes, which would continue for four years and culminate in ordination as a priest, began shortly after they arrived. (First-year students had nine courses: General Church History to A.D. 325, the year of the Council of Nicea, which codified Christianity and produced the Nicene Creed; English Church History, (a) Earliest Times to 1066, (b) 1066–1509; Old Testament; Pastoral Theology; New Testament Introduction; Canon of Holy Scripture; The Prayer Book I; History of the Creeds; and

Patristics, the study of Early Christian writers and their works, in this case Augustine's *De Fide et Symbolo*—the Faith and the Creed—in Latin.) From May through September, the students left the classroom to gain practical experience in mission churches where there was no resident rector, to serve under the direction of a neighboring priest. This entailed a tremendous amount of bumpy travel by Model T Ford over bald—roadless—prairie. As my father had heretofore not driven a car, the open space was probably a good thing. In all, he tended to the spiritual needs of several hundred people spread over about 4,500 square miles of general emptiness to the east, west, and south of Regina.

By the time I was ten, I had heard a lot about my father's seminary days, at least those stories that had a vaguely antic quality. He told me of the May day shortly after he had settled in for his second summer's work when, while talking with the manager of the lumberyard in the town where he would live when not on the road, an officer of the Royal Canadian Mounted Police came in and asked the manager straightaway, "How much lumber does it take to make a coffin?" Once that was settled and someone set to constructing one, the Mountie asked where he could find an Anglican priest.

"Right here," the manager said, introducing my father.

Without ado, the Mountie said, "I want you to come with me and bury a man."

It would be the first funeral my father conducted. When the rough casket was finished, he and the Mountie loaded it up and drove out to the house where the elderly farmer had been found dead, sitting on the edge of his bed. He was the first of many corpses my father would see in his ministry, and he never forgot the surprise he felt at the gurgle that came from the dead man's throat when they laid him out. The Mountie rounded up a few neighbors to help dig the grave, which was not easy, because a couple of feet below the surface, the ground was still frozen from the winter's frost, which went down many feet. Finally a shallow hole deep enough to lower the casket was hacked out. When my father was ready to begin the service, he discovered he could not find a hymn that everyone knew. What everyone could agree on was that it was not fitting to bury a man without one, so a neighbor went home to get his windup gramophone and a recording of favorite hymns. It was dark when he returned, and by lantern light the service was said, the hymn played, the coffin buried, and a pile of stones put atop the grave to protect it from hungry animals.

Because people were sparsely settled on the prairie and Greek Orthodox priests were rarer even than Anglican ones, the Orthodox bishop asked that my father and his colleagues officiate as necessary for his congregants. Thus my father found himself one day leading the procession to the graveside for an Orthodox funeral. A fair way into the churchyard, he had a sudden feeling that he was alone. Looking behind him, he saw the family had stopped near the gate and were gathered around the coffin, which they had stood upright and had opened, having their picture taken standing beside the deceased.

Then there was the day he found a crate containing bottles of homemade whiskey behind the altar in one of the

missions he tended, near the U.S. border. (There was Prohibition in the States but not in Canada, and my father's
territory crossed the border when communities were near
it. So did the rumrunners.) Amused, he showed the cache
to a Mountie friend, who, equally amused, said he knew
who had made it. They arranged to serve it at a card game,
which the moonshiner attended, not knowing he was
drinking his own concoction, though they didn't drink it
all. It was winter, so the Mountie gave my father several
bottles to use as antifreeze in his car.

The subtext of many of these stories was that privation
and having to make do were integral to understanding my
father's worldview. This was during the Depression; har-
vests were meager—a regular reply from a farmer asked
about his crops was that he had "nothing of everything"—
and cash more so, which meant my father was often paid
in food rather than in dollars and it was not uncommon to
come home and find a crate of twelve dozen eggs on the
porch. Axle grease sold for five or six cents a pound,
unsalted homemade butter for a penny or two less, so
farmers gave him butter to use on his car.

Prairie winters were staggeringly cold. During one six-
week stretch, my father said, the temperature never rose
above minus 40 degrees Fahrenheit, and one morning he
awoke in the town of Cardross (it had a grain elevator, a
bank, and a church, but not much else), where he was
temporarily stationed, to find his roommate, a bank teller,
dropping eggs on the floor without their breaking. They
had frozen solid in the night because one of them had for-
gotten to stoke the furnace before going to bed.

As I became more and more familiar with the rites and

rituals of the Episcopal Church, often explained and detailed to me by my father, I more and more appreciated and believed in their sanctity and their historical legitimacy. The languages of the services may have been translated over a period of two thousand years, but their meaning and import did not change. Prime among these rites are the two steps a novitiate must go through to become a priest. After the required three years of preparation, my father was ordained deacon in April 1932, the first of these steps. Deacons, though they receive Holy Orders by the laying on of hands from a bishop, are ordained to service rather than to the priesthood and spend about a year in a sort of probationary period, doing most of the work of a priest save for the absolution of sins and baptizing people (though they can do the later in extreme circumstances). After that period, a deacon again comes before a bishop to be ordained a priest by someone whom the Anglican, Roman Catholic, and several Orthodox denominations believe is in the apostolic succession, which is to say that bishops can trace their succession back to the twelve apostles, and thus the bishop who lays his hands on the head of a deacon to ordain him or her a priest is passing sanctification uninterrupted for two millennia.

My father's eleven months as a deacon were spent doing additional course work at St. Chad's as well as offering short-term help to priests and parishes where needed; in my father's case, one stop was in Moosomin to assist the rector of St. Alban's Church. (Saint Alban was the first English Christian martyr, a formerly pagan Roman soldier who sheltered a priest wanted by the authorities. The priest converted Alban and baptized him, and when soldiers came to Alban's house in their search, he put on the priest's robe and allowed himself to be arrested. When the deception was discovered, the furious magistrate decreed that Alban should suffer the same punishment meant for the priest, and he was beheaded, probably in A.D. 304. I go into such detail because, as will become evident, parishes named for Saint Alban played a large role in my family's life.)

Two of the parishioners at St. Alban's were William Gabb, the proprietor of a local hotel, and his wife, Mabel, herself raised in Wentworth, only three miles from my father's village. In the late 1890s, Will went with a cousin of Mabel's to South Africa to open a hardware business that catered to the flood of gold and diamond miners. In 1901, he returned to England to marry Mabel and then went by himself to homestead in Saskatchewan; once he was settled, he sent for her.

In 1907, Will and Mabel had a daughter, Dorothy, a beauty who loved going to church and was deeply drawn to its teaching. A graduate of the nursing school at Winnipeg General Hospital, 170 miles away, she stayed on as a registered nurse, earning five dollars for a twelve-hour shift, when she could get one. In the living room of Will and Mabel's suite in their hotel was a graduation photo of her in her white uniform and cap, holding a bouquet of yellow roses. Five-four, with wavy brown hair and hazel eyes, she looked rather like Ingrid Bergman. My father, five-six and thin, with wavy brown hair himself and mirthful brown eyes, looked considerably like Stan Laurel.

(When I was a kid, my father would jokingly say to people of me, "He has his mother's looks. I still have mine.")

It's a simple story from here, one that I always enjoyed listening to, because courtship and life on the prairie were so far removed from what I knew, they could have been in another galaxy. Will and Mabel liked my father and invited him to the hotel, where he saw the picture of Dorothy and thought, That's the girl I'm going to marry. Mabel, meanwhile, wrote to Dorothy about the nice young priest— and from Elsecar!—saying, "I know you'll like him."

Indeed she did, but the depth of his feelings was clearer to him than hers were to her. They walked, they played tennis, they drove the prairie. About a month after they met, my father was assigned to assist in a new parish. The night before he left, he told Dorothy that he loved her. She, cautious, protected (as a girl, she was not allowed to cross the railroad tracks that divided the eight-block town), and not experienced with romance, proposed to be his friend. (My father was less cautious and protected; he had come out to Canada, after all, and had known love at least once.) Over the next months he wrote often, always adding that he loved her. She wrote back, never saying she loved him. Then, four months into this exchange, she realized she did. They were engaged, but it was two and a half years before they married. For one thing, my father needed a permanent job.

In March 1933, he was ordained a priest, and eventually he and Dorothy were married in St. Alban's Church, where she had been confirmed in 1922. During my childhood, they often made reference to their life before I was

born, and I pictured them in the tiny churches in the small
towns with the odd names on the endless prairie. Following their wedding, they stopped for lunch in Indian Head
on the way to a two-night honeymoon in Moose Jaw. Then
they settled into the rectory in Mossbank, the smaller of
the two towns that comprised my father's new parish. The
house had no running water. A tank in the cellar gathered
rainwater, but for everyday usage, they collected water at
a pump in town. A few months later, they moved to Assini-
boia, the larger town of the parish—about fifteen hundred
people—where they lived in a newer house, this one with
its own water. The house was the last on the street. Beyond
the backyard fence was nothing but prairie, which provided a clear path for all the dust blowing north from the
ravaged American farmlands of the Dust Bowl years. In
the winter, their house was the first interference for icy
arctic air that had whipped along for hundreds of miles
unimpeded by anything. During the long winters there
was little to do between services and visits to invalids.
There was a curling rink in town. At home there was a
radio the size of a small bookcase that provided virtually
all their entertainment and news; I grew up seeing a picture of them beside it, their cocker spaniel asleep at their
feet. They looked contented. Both loved Gilbert and Sulli-
van. They had a set of 78-rpm recordings and each had a
leather-bound book of Gilbert's lyrics to follow along
with, and their delight was passed on to me. Both enjoyed
cribbage, which my mother had learned aurally as a young
girl. Her bedroom was above the living room, and the
heating pipe carried the voices of her father and friends

counting variants of "fifteen two, fifteen four, two are six and three are nine" as they added their combinations of fifteen, their pairs, and their runs. During the long prairie winters my parents played many, many series of best-of-101 games, and from my early childhood on, I often played with one or both of them.

Considering the physical, geographic, and economic hardships they faced, it was fortunate for the Anglican Church as well as for them that their marriage was a twofer. My mother even then was more devout than my father, and she was a strict constructionist when it came to theology. I think her piety and faith were a comfort as well as a shield against the troubles of the world. As my father had gone on spiritual journeys with the monks at Mirfield, my mother was an associate member of the Sisterhood of St. John the Divine, an order of nuns founded in 1884 in Toronto, which ran St. Chad's School for Girls and whose members take vows of chastity, obedience, and service. (Fortunately for me, associate members are not required to take the first vow.) She became involved as she grew to know the seminary through my father, and for all her life thereafter, she wore a silver cross around her neck, with "SSJD" engraved on one side and "God Is Love" on the other. Their mutual faith helped them through the winters and brought some solace to my mother in her perpetual fight against severe hay fever.

Her allergy prompted the bishop to move them to the residential school on the George Gordon First Nation Reserve, a forty-eight-square-mile Indian reserve not far from Moosomin, which might provide at least a slightly better environment.

As with the Indians in the United States, those in Canada had been exiled to reservations, their cultures equally mauled. My father, hopeful of being helpful to the Cree and Salteaux people of Gordon, took the position of chaplain. He led a service every morning for the students in the school and took Sunday services in the neighboring town of Punnichy, which was easy enough to get to in summer but required a one-horse sleigh in winter. My father's relations with Chief George, whose grandfather, known as Chief Kawacatoose, signed a treaty in 1874 that allocated one square mile to each family of five, were in marked contrast to those of the white Indian agent and his wife, who intensely disliked their posting and their charges. My father became quite friendly with the chief, who understood his intentions I don't think my father was entirely free of the English notion of Kipling's "White Man's burden" but he saw everyone as a person. I have a small photo of the chief and his wife hanging next to the beaded and fringed elk-skin tobacco pouch that he gave to my father as a farewell present when he and my mother moved on after a year.

It is quite likely that he would have stayed a priest on the prairie for his entire career were it not for my mother's hay fever, which grew worse with each passing year and set them on a journey to find a more suitable climate. The first stop was a sparsely settled area north of Vancouver, British Columbia, where Will and Mabel were now settled. I was born there in 1944, ten months after my father's nephew Eric was killed with all his fellow crew when their Royal Air Force Halifax plane crashed on landing after having been damaged during a training run on which he had volunteered to help. My birth after nine

Family portrait, 1948

years of marriage—my mother was thirty-seven, my father forty—was considered something of a minor miracle, especially in its timing with regard to my namesake's death. But the hay fever continued, and so when I was three, we moved to Southern California, where, at last, there was a climate that virtually ended it.

My father became the curate, or associate rector, at Christ Church in Coronado, an island a half mile across the bay from San Diego. The rector of the relatively affluent parish was an elderly man not many years from retirement. Apparently, he was independently wealthy, because he and his wife lived not in the beautiful wooden two-story, five-bedroom rectory next to the stone, peaked slate-roofed church with its glorious Tiffany stained-glass windows and a carillon, but, rather, in a home of their own several blocks away. That was just fine with my parents, who had never lived in so grand a place.

My father was an immediate hit with the congregation.

He lived a life of evident faith yet was not pious about it: He could preach without being preachy. He also led services for children. At one in 1948, he used the plague of frogs in chapter 8 of Exodus as the basis for his homily about not complaining. Reading it now, it seems he must have sounded like Mary Poppins in a clerical collar.

"Imagine," he said to the kids, aged five to nine,

frogs everywhere. In drinking water, in the bread-mixing bowl, in bed, on tables, underfoot so that the Egyptians slipped on them. Frogs in their shoes, in their clothes. No one dared drink water because it was full of frogs. Frogs were everywhere, right into the Pharaoh's palace. It was very miserable. "Croak croak—croak" all day and night. People didn't notice the sun shining because all they could think about was the croaking of frogs.

Lots of boys and girls are like that! They cannot see the good things in life for croaking—we call it *grumbling*! How they croak! They cannot do *anything*. They grumble at this, at that—"It's too hot"; "It's too cold." If we cannot get our own way, we grumble at that, too! We grumble when our parents ask us to do things. . . .

One of my father's duties was to work with the youth group, which, because of his easy humor and affinity for young people, grew in size and popularity once he took it over. He worried about morals and Christian teaching and living, and he set the tone for good behavior in sermons, homilies, and counseling. But to him, *Christian* did not mean dour, and good-natured fun was always part of the equation. "I'm a firm believer in the two-party system," he once deadpanned to a group of teenagers who were talking about politics, "one on Friday, and another on Saturday." Many older congregants also took to this newcomer with his English accent, attractive wife, and young son. There are several family photos of us on the rectory lawn, surrounded by palm trees and flowering bushes. After the barren prairie, Coronado was like Eden for my parents. And as in Eden, human frailty changed everything.

Three years after our arrival, the rector called my father from Florida, where he was looking for a retirement home, to say that, effective at the end of the month, my father's services were no longer necessary. He offered no reason save that one priest was now enough for the parish. Members of the Junior Women's Auxiliary, upset by my parents' leaving, chipped in to buy a large silver tray engraved with their words of thanks. The bishop had no posting available on such short notice, and so at the end of May 1950 the three of us and our cocker spaniel drove back to British Columbia, in the hope that the bishop there would have an opening. We would stay with my grandparents until something came along. My sixth-birthday dinner was in a roadside café in Oregon, where my parents managed to get a cake decorated with "Happy Birthday" and seven candles—one to grow on. I knew nothing about the cause of this sudden travel, as my parents kept their disappointment and worry well concealed. But neither did they know exactly why.

In the film *The Bishop's Wife,* David Niven is a bishop so fixated on the idea of a new cathedral and so manipulated by a wealthy old widow whom he sees as the purse for his venture that in frustration he prays for help, which arrives in the form of Cary Grant as an angel named Dudley in a well-tailored suit. While the bishop continues in his quest for money for the cathedral at the expense of time with his wife, daughter, and parishioners in the small city churches that comprise the diocese, Dudley wins the affection of all. The bishop, suddenly seeing what has happened, commands Dudley to leave. Because it's a Christmas movie, following another couple of twists and turns there is a happy ending. The bishop sees the error of his ways, severs the strings the widow has used to control him, is reunited in affection with his family, and preaches his Christmas Eve sermon in the lowliest of the churches.

In my father's case, there was no satisfyingly neat ending. It would be several years before he knew the story of his dismissal. Then one day the rector telephoned my father to apologize and to ask his forgiveness. The priest admitted to my father that he had been distracted by his impending retirement, and then he suddenly saw that the affections and loyalty of much of his congregation had shifted to the younger man, who was always available. He realized what he had lost and fired my father out of jealousy. My father forgave the old man, and in several talks we had about the event after I learned about it as an adult, he expressed no resentment or anger, merely sadness (he and my mother really liked Coronado) tempered by an understanding of human nature. My father had by then built a strong parish in a small town of far less wealth and he and my mother were happy there. "The Lord works in mysterious ways," he said in many circumstances, and this was one of them. What has stayed with me is how he used his faith to put his disappointment and hurt into a perspective that eased them, and how his own sense of vocation was not altered by the failure of someone like himself, sworn and ordained to lead and preach a Christian life, to do so. For me, it was this capability to understand and accept that all humans have weaknesses and not to judge those who transgressed in small or large ways that made him the priest he was. He believed the Christian tenet that humans are born into sin and moral error, and therefore both are entirely to be expected. The only way out of them is through redemption by the one person my father believed to have lived a perfect life.

When I was seventeen, I put this belief to a test. While driving on the freeway to see friends on a Saturday night, I was given a ticket for going eight miles an hour over the posted limit of fifty-five. I knew my father would be upset with me, and then I had an idea.

"Dad," I said when I got home, "isn't it true that we're all sinners?"

"Yes," he replied.

"And isn't it true that if we're truly sorry for our sins, we are forgiven?"

"Yes," he said again, unsure where this was leading.

"Well, I did this and I'm truly sorry," I said, handing him the ticket.

He burst into laughter. Then a few seconds later, he said in all seriousness, "Don't do it again."

It was not the bishop in British Columbia, who had baptized me and, although a good friend to my father, was about to retire, but the bishop of the Diocese of Los Angeles who offered my father a parish. A month after we left Coronado, a letter came saying there was a church in Eagle Rock, in the eastern part of Los Angeles, which could use someone temporarily while a more permanent placement was sought. In late 1950, a few months after we settled in at Holy Angels, my father was visited by a young doctor from the mission church St. Alban's in the San Diego suburb of El Cajon, a town then of about five thousand people, fifteen miles into what was at the time almost entirely open country covered by many live oak, eucalyptus, and pepper trees, and even more scrub brush. (Missions are supported by the diocese; parishes are self-sufficient.) A week or two after an interview and dinner, the doctor wrote to ask on behalf of the few score congregants if my father would come and be their rector, which he did in April 1951. The doctor and his wife had three young children, the eldest son my age, and our families quickly became very close. My mother worked part-time in the doctor's office, as well. For many years, our two families celebrated Thanksgiving, Christmas, New Year's, and Easter together and saw each other often, and most weekends I spent at least one day at their house, playing with their kids.

Then, during the civil rights movement of the 1960s, came one of the hardest decisions my father said he ever had to make, which pitted a priest's duty against friendship. The doctor, born and raised in the South, was increasingly vocal about his belief that blacks were inferior to whites. He called them "niggers" and he spoke with anger and spite about Martin Luther King, Jr., and other leaders. The Episcopal Church was an early and enthusiastic supporter of the movement, and my father wished he had taken part in the voter-registration drives and the marches from Selma to Montgomery, Alabama, in 1965. My father talked—argued, for that matter—often with his dear friend, telling him that his behavior was unChristian and sinful, and that before one came to the altar rail to receive Communion, he had to acknowledge his sins and ask God's forgiveness. He made no progress. I remember my father's anguish when he told me about this as it was going on, yet he knew he had no choice. Finally my father told his friend and parishioner that he could not in good conscience give him Communion if his heart was so full of hate and no effort was made to overcome his prejudices. Rather than do that, the doctor, who had been steadily generous to the parish and to our family, left the congregation and became a Roman Catholic. He and my father did not speak for several years.

Three

Although my father never said so directly, he would have been thrilled if I had decided to become a priest. My doing so, of course, would have been dependent on my feeling called to the ministry, and he did everything he could to ensure my spiritual ears were always open. When we moved to El Cajon, I began my career as an acolyte. There were none before we arrived and I was among the first four he trained. At six, I was just old enough to be able to remember all there was to do in the service and I liked doing it well. For the first couple of years, I was always the acolyte for the 7:30 service because, as other boys joined, they and their families preferred to come to the more sensibly timed family service at 9:15 or the almost entirely adult one at 11:00. Just before a service was scheduled to start, my father would check his watch, I would surreptitiously look to be sure the congregation was seated, and then we would walk out of what doubled as his office and the sacristy as the congregation came to its feet. We continued along in front of the Communion rail and entered the chancel midway, at which point the congregation knelt. I took my place on the step to the left of the altar.

"The Lord be with you," my father said, facing the congregation, his arms outstretched, his forearms and hands pointing upward.

"And with thy spirit," the congregation responded.

"Let us pray." And he turned to the altar and began reading from the missal, the 1928 version of the Book of Common Prayer, the last to use Cranmer's lifting language. In 1979, the words of the service and everything else in the prayer book were rendered in current English usage. Majestic gave way to commonplace. (The 1928 service of Holy Communion is included in the book, but very few parishes use it, and rather follow the new version, called "Rite II.")

These early services had an almost metronomic pace, the only parts slightly longer or shorter being the length of the Epistle and Gospel readings and an additional prayer at Easter, which generally amounted to a swing on one end or the other of perhaps a minute. My period of light-headedness and vomiting was two years in coming and lasted five or six weeks before its cause was discerned. I think it continued as long as it did in part because I was worried that it would happen and the power of suggestion took over. In the meantime, while my mind often wandered as the service progressed, I never missed a cue for my next action. I was alert when it was time to count the parishioners and prepare the Elements. I liked the conspiratorial feeling of the tallying and whispering and the silent hand-

The first four acolytes (Eric second from right), 1952

ing off of the ciborium and the cruets. I also liked accepting the collection plate from the usher who had passed it among the faithful and then brought it to the altar for blessing. The amount in the pledge envelopes in the plates at that time was not substantial, but being with my father and the treasurer in the office after a service, counting it out and noting it down, I felt a consummate insider.

We were a pair, my father and I, at the altar. When people said complimentary things about me to my father, he would call me "a chip off the old block." (When, in my teens, I grew to be six inches taller than him, I became "a block off the old chip.") Although there soon were many acolytes, I was the one to help him for services that fell on days other than Sunday, which pleased me, because I felt I was at once doing something special with him that also was routine. We did things together away from church—we watched the Friday-night fights on TV, played golf, and went to ball games—but at the altar we were like dance partners, each of whom knew the other's steps before he made them.

When there was a wedding, we each carried a worry into the marriage service. Mine, as I mentioned earlier, was that the bride would not be able to get the ring onto the groom's finger. My father's had greater import. It was that after he said, "If any man can show just cause, why they may not lawfully be joined together, let him now speak, or else hereafter for ever hold his peace," someone would call out "I can!" Or that after he told the bride and groom, "I require and charge you both, as ye will answer at the dreadful day of judgment when the secrets of all hearts shall be disclosed, that if either of you know any impediment, why ye may not be lawfully joined together in Matrimony, ye do now confess it. For be ye well assured, that if any persons are joined together otherwise than as God's Word doth allow, their marriage is not lawful," one would fess up. It never happened.

My comfort in church extended to being in the congregation. When I was perhaps seven, I joined my parents at a service at the largest church in San Diego, which brought together many parishes. The pews were full and we were seated in the loft at the back. I had just learned to read, and as we all sang the hymns, I discovered how to follow the words and match them to the notes. I felt a surge of pride, which increased as I basked in my parents' expressed delight.

For my father, the tiny mission church with a congregation of less than one hundred was nearly a reiteration of his work on the prairie. The frontier sensibility of the town—at least as much frontier as there could be in Southern California—was beguiling. There was a lot of open space, including across from one side of the church, and within a three-minute drive to the east you were in the country, where one of the parishioners had a riding stable. The difference was that this California town, unlike those static places in Saskatchewan, was set to grow rapidly in the postwar housing boom that filled American suburbs. As El Cajon grew, so did St. Alban's. (The city is pronounced *el ka-hone*. The translation from Spanish is "the box," which is apt, because the ocean breezes that cooled San Diego and other towns on the relatively flat plain in from the coast could not dip down into the enclosed valley, which always was hotter by fifteen degrees or more.)

It was common for my father to make house calls to the ill and shut-ins, and he was available at all hours in an emergency. He received a dispensation from the police department to have a spotlight mounted near the outside mirror of his car so he could find house addresses in the dark. The doctor who was instrumental in bringing us to El Cajon also made house calls day and night. I felt there was a certain kinship in how they approached their jobs, though as was evident in the doctor's lovely home, one certainly paid better than the other. St. Alban's had no rectory when we arrived, so a small two-bedroom place just around the circle from the church was rented for us; it was about a sixth the size of our home in Coronado and lacked the charm, but that was offset by the excitement of a new town and church. A year after we arrived, a comfortable one-story, three-bedroom rectory of about twelve hundred square feet was built on the church property. It would be our family home until my father's retirement seventeen years later.

I had nearly completed second grade when we came to El Cajon, and my parents quickly enrolled me at the St. Andrews parish school in La Mesa, three miles away. My father drove me there every day. He quickly became close with the Reverend C. Boone Sadler, the rector, in part because each of them understood the challenges the other faced in turning a mission into a self-sustaining parish in a small town, but mainly, I think, because their personalities and outlooks on life were ideally suited. After I ran off to class, the two of them, clad in their gray or black suits and clerical collars, went into the church to say Morning Prayer together.

Both Boone and my father cared deeply about young people and both were heavily involved with a church camp in the mountains, seventy-five miles east of San Diego. (Many Episcopal dioceses had camps in the 1950s.) They saw camping as an almost stealthy means of Christian education: Take some kids, put them in the great outdoors, where for a week they can have fun and incidentally contemplate God's universe by just looking up at night, have a chapel service in the morning and a campfire at night with songs and skits, and you've improved their chances of leading an upright life. Religion was a part of it, but not hard-sell indoctrination. And the campers loved it. I know, because I was part of it every summer between the ages of eight and nineteen.

In 1951, shortly after we moved to El Cajon, the camp in the Cuyamaca Mountains east of San Diego that Boone had for years been a big part of was destroyed in a forest fire. He immediately set to finding another site, and my father joined him. Eventually they found what they felt was an ideal place, also in the Cuyamacas, near the town of Julian, at an elevation of about five thousand feet. It was sixty-six acres of live and black oaks, manzanita bushes, and Coulter pines. There were forested hills and valley meadows as well as flat areas suitable for building. The only structures on the property at the time were four one-room cabins and a larger building with several rooms. The price was twenty thousand dollars.

Boone and my father signed a letter of agreement with the owner, though at the time they had less than five hundred dollars between them and not a cent committed by the diocese to buy or support a camp. Maybe it was their clerical collars and guileless faces that lulled the owner into signing away his land without checking out the buyers, but whatever the reason, he did. Perhaps this is a lesson in faith.

It was certainly a lesson in anxiety. Boone and my father talked often on the phone, and several nights a month Boone would show up at our house at nine or ten o'clock and the two would have a drink and share problems or just talk and laugh. Boone called my father "Jackson," and after they had signed the agreement for the camp he sometimes wondered what they had gotten into. "Jackson," he once lamented, only half in jest, "we could go to jail!" In the end, a generous widow and a few other individuals contributed enough to get the camp going, and the diocese added funds as well and quickly assumed responsibility for its upkeep. It was named Camp Stevens, in honor of a deceased bishop of the Diocese of Los Angeles who had been a big fan of camping programs.

The army-surplus tents we slept in the first couple of years were replaced by six-bed A-frames on Boys Hill and, across a gulley, more on Girls Hill. Nat "King" Cole, an Episcopalian, gave the proceeds from a concert to build a dining hall. A swimming pool was added. Days began with a chapel service and ended with a campfire at which there were corny skits and sing-alongs.

One was biblical fun:

Salome was a dancer, she danced the hootchie-kootch
She danced before the king and she didn't wear too mooch
The king, being ruler, said, "We'll have no scandal here!"
But Salome said, "The heck we won't," and kicked the chandelier.

Another, when I was older, was mock denominational chauvinism, to the tune of "God Bless America":

I am an Anglican.
I'm a P. E.
Not a high church,
Nor a low church,
But a Protestant Episcopal and free.
Not a Lutheran,
Nor a Presby,
Nor a Baptist, white with foam.
I am an Anglican,

Just one step from Rome.
I am an Anglican,
Just one step from Rome.

(Episcopalians like inside jokes about themselves. They also tend to feel a cocktail is a welcome part of communal activity. A line in the Prayer of Saint Chrysostom in the service of Evensong is: "When two or three are gathered together in thy Name thou wilt grant their requests. . . ." A variant reference goes: "When three or four Episcopalians are gathered together, you'll usually find a fifth.")

And always at the end, no matter our age, there was the camp song, set to the tune of "The Bells of St. Mary's." What strikes me about it today is how it exactly mirrored the intentions of Boone and my father and the others who were committed to making the camp a place to take those who wished to come closer to God:

All hail to Camp Stevens
Our memories are of you
Your tall pines, your great oaks
Your valleys so deep.

Where God walks beside us
And youth is invited
To hear the call, to know the Christ
And make Him known.

Then in the dark and almost always under a clear moon and starlit sky, we turned on our flashlights and walked the dusty road a quarter of a mile to the A-frames. Girls Hill came first, and during the weeks when there were mid-teenage campers, there would be couples who held hands along the way and kissed each other good night on the road. The adult staff (always one or two priests, who were the deans, and a nurse) kept a respectful distance and interfered only if things started getting out of hand. It was on that road, when I was fifteen or sixteen, that I first kissed a girl, a glancing blow that lasted a nanosecond but reverberated in me for hours.

Camp sessions ran from Sunday afternoon to Saturday after breakfast. Friday night was a quiet night, with no talking after the campfire until we spoke our parts the next morning in the service of Holy Communion held in the open chapel in a clearing in the woods down a dirt road that started at the end of the swimming pool. Fallen logs served as pews; the altar was more or less sheltered by an A-frame, which we could look through to the trees and mountain behind it. The quiet night was meant to be a time to reflect on the week and to allow us to better absorb God's grandeur in nature and to listen for Him in our prayers. What usually happened was a great deal of sign language and barely suppressed laughter in the communal toilet/shower building and then amid the beams of the flashlights once we were in bed. But there were occasions when something happened. I don't discount the power of the emotion engendered in the evening, but during at least one of those nights in my early teens I felt particularly close to God as I drifted to sleep, and woke up in the morning thinking I would become a priest.

*Eric (lower left) among the counselors
at Camp Stevens, ca. 1961*

My father was involved with overseeing the running of
the camp until he died, and he spent part of every summer
there. I was a camper, then a counselor, and for three years
I was one of the permanent staff, for two of them the lifeguard. I roamed the deck of the twenty-five-by-fifty-foot
pool, blowing my whistle at rowdy kids and getting a tan,
which by July made me invisible when I stood against the
redwood fence that hid the filter and other machinery.
(Other lifeguard duties included hauling trash to the
dump and doing whatever labor-intensive chores the
camp director decided needed doing.)

Occasionally during my permanent summer staff years,
my father and I were there at the same time, which I found
to be a great treat, though I was discomfited one evening
when he discovered me necking with a girl on staff with
whom I was having a summer romance. Actually, he might
have been more uncomfortable than I, because other than

the surprise and then the smile he showed at the time as he hastily got out of the way, he never mentioned it.

Death was a regular part of my father's work, but that seldom registered with me until I was nine and my maternal grandparents moved to El Cajon on short notice. My grandfather had been diagnosed with breast cancer so advanced, there was no treatment to offer. His health was rapidly failing, and caring for him became too much for my grandmother.

We had only recently moved into the new rectory. My grandmother and mother took turns tending my grandfather, under the watchful care of our doctor friend. For all my life, my grandfather had been a bon vivant who dazzled me with his card shuffling, and he promised to give me ten dollars once he'd decided I could handle a deck properly. I practiced hard and he paid up when I was eight. But now he no longer resembled the man I had known all my life. He was terribly thin, his skin was papery, with no color, and he smelled ill. I went in to see him a couple of times a day, but it was difficult. About all I could do was show off my shuffle. On the day after Christmas, five or six weeks after his arrival, he died.

My father liked the local mortician. He felt the undertaker did not prey on grief and that he conducted his business respectably. It was at the mortuary that I would see my grandfather for the first time since his death. My parents had not wanted me to see his body in bed, as they felt it might be too upsetting to me. In fact, they had sent me on a specious errand as he was dying. Before we went to the mortuary, my father explained what the room in

which we would see the body would be like. He told me
the casket would be open and that my grandfather would
look like he was sleeping, even though he would be
dressed in a suit. He reminded me that although his body
was dead, his soul still lived and that I should not look on
this as the end of him. I could say something if I wanted, or
just offer a silent prayer. He warned me that my mother
and grandmother might cry.

We went to the mortuary, and it was as my father said it
would be. My grandfather lay in the casket in a small
room. I knew from studying my catechism and listening to
my father's sermons that the death of the body was not the
death of the soul, but this was the first time I had to put
teaching into perspective, and it was hard for me to separate the life of my grandfather's soul from his inert,
embalmed body.

A few years later, my father preached a sermon that was
reminiscent of how my grandfather was treated in our
home. It was given on one of the seven Sundays after
Easter, during the period of fifty days between Easter and
Pentecost, the day that the Holy Spirit descended on the
apostles and other followers of Jesus Christ. (The liturgi-
cal season corresponds to the Jewish seven-week period
between Passover and Shavuot, which commemorates
both the harvest of the first fruit and the celebration of the
giving of the Torah on Mount Sinai.) It began:

In the last fifty years, the world has changed more
than in all the years since it was formed. Of all the
scientists born into the world, seventy percent are
alive today, and changes are still being made. This has

caused a revision in our mode of life, until we can hardly recognize the world of yesterday. This change is best observed in our homes and daily lives.

We have changed from a home-centered community to a centralized community, in ways that are not at first apparent. Fifty years ago, children were born in the home, were sick in bed at home, died at home, and were then taken to the church and buried in a churchyard, which was part of the church, and a natural part.

Now, children are born in hospitals, we go to hospitals when we are sick, die in hospitals, and are buried from a funeral home. When we become senior citizens, we no longer grow old gracefully in the bosom of our family, but we go to a Senior Citizens Home, where, among old people, we never hear the sound of children's voices, and then to a nursing home, where we die among strangers, or else to a hospital, where death comes to us.

In consequence, the realities of life—growing old and dying—are hidden from our children, and I frequently have to deal with young married people who have never had any dealings with death, or serious sickness, and are terrified of both. Children are suddenly confronted with the fact that grandma has disappeared, and then realize that this will also happen to them. Death is a terrifying mystery, and is treated as such.

This is true of the modern funeral, when everything helps to deepen the mystery. There is the family room, where the relatives may be alone with their grief. Gone is the day when the neighbors were there to help. A curtain separates the family from the other mourners. The coffin is brought in from a slumber room. As an ungrammatical speaker said not long ago, "Who's kidding who?" At the graveside, the grave is draped with a green cloth—we must not see the grave, which is far worse than an honest hole with earth around it. Everybody knows what is going to happen, but we kid ourselves by being mysterious. Even the age-old custom of throwing earth on the coffin has been disguised. The priest is handed a glass container, full of sterile sand, guaranteed not to make an unpleasant sound when it hits the coffin.

The whole purpose of the burial is to point out that death is as natural as being born, and now the body is returning to its original dust. But we don't even let *that* happen. Everything is done to preserve a useless body. We embalm it; it is placed in a coffin lined with satin, which is then placed in a cement box or a bronze vault. You may read ads in the papers showing these vaults, with the caption, "Is your loved one lying in water?" or some such thing. Nor should we blame the funeral director for these things.

Many people have no church affiliations, and, when faced with death, can look no further than the fact that a loved one has created a loss in their lives, and they want to hang on to the physical body for as long as possible, because they see no soul. To them, death and decay are dreadful things. They want to hide the facts, disguise the grave, make a show of flowers, sing a sentimental song (usually "The Old Rugged Cross," which they have ignored all their lives). The funeral director has to deal with many more non-Christians, or nominal Christians, than any other group of people, and this is what they want and the director has to go along with it.

But to the Christian, all this is wrong.

First. Let us tell our children when they ask about death that it is a natural thing, the natural ending to life on Earth, but that it is the opening of a door into a richer life, one that will continue forever—that death is, in fact, a mere incident in our life. Should they ask further questions, tell them that the purpose of burial is to dispose of a body for which there is no further use, but as this body has been the house of a soul, the *real* person, who thought and smiled and did kind things, we must bury it with decency and reverence. Repeat that the person is still alive, but without the body, and that when we knew him on Earth we only saw the results of his real self. His face smiled because his soul was kind, not his body; and now his real self—the soul—is gone from the body, free forever from pain, sorrow, grief, and unkindness. . . .

Throughout our house there were, I realize now, many references to physical death and the promise of life for the soul. Even the wall calendar was church-related. The dates on the Episcopal Church Kalender (it employs the ancient spelling) are colored according to the ecclesiastical season, the same way a priest's robes are colored—purple for Lent and Advent, white for Easter, and so forth. Most walls in

the rectory had something hanging on them, but the art-
work was minimal. The exception was in the living room,
where there was a quite lovely desertscape in oil paint
done by one of the nurses my mother worked with in our
friend the doctor's office. The nurse seldom came to
church, and her husband never did, but one day when I was
eleven or so my father asked if I would be the acolyte for a
private baptism he was doing that afternoon. Just before
the service, I discovered the person to be baptized was the
husband of the nurse. Apparently, he had come to my father
with questions about the teachings of the Church and one
discussion led to another, and now here he was, in his
fifties, ready to take the plunge, as it were. As there were
just the three of us, we joked that I was his godfather.

Otherwise, the walls of the rectory held photos   one
was a large black-and-white photo of a priest standing in
the apse of a cathedral, light from a tall window shining on
him, his head bowed as he reads his prayer book—and several pieces of religious iconography. There was a crucifix
on one wall in my parents' room and one in mine as well,
plus another in the dining room. In the hallway leading to
the bedrooms and bathroom there was a nine-by-twelve-
inch reproduction of the Victorian artist William Holman
Hunt's *The Light of the World,* a representation of Jesus holding a candle lantern, knocking on a door partially overgrown with vines. (The door is said to represent the human
conscience.) I thought it a rather sentimental painting at
the time and find it almost kitsch today, though it is a powerful picture for many and was for my parents. Beside it
was a framed sheet of calligraphy in the style of an illumi-

nated Bible, done by my father, a good artist, of the first half of "The Gate of the Year" by the English writer Minnie Louise Haskins (1875–1957). The poem became popular throughout the British Empire after King George VI quoted it in a radio broadcast to his subjects, a program that my parents listened to after Britain declared war on Germany in 1939. It begins with the poet asking the man who is by the gate for a light as she ventures forth into the unseen. The man responds:

"Go into the darkness and put your hand into the hand
    of God.
That shall be to you better than light and safer than a
    known way!"

Also in my parents' room was a similar-size picture of Jesus' head, His face bearded and a crown of thorns in His long hair. It was a lithograph of Gabriel Max's *St. Veronica's Handkerchief.* (Veronica was one of the holy women of Jerusalem who followed Jesus to Calvary. She gave Him a cloth to wipe His face, and many believe its imprint was left upon it.) Depending on how you shift your head, as you look at the painting, the eyes open and shut. ("Fourteen colors were used to get this remarkable effect," a note at the bottom of the lithograph explains.) My mother bought it as a nursing student in Winnipeg and had kept it on a wall wherever she'd lived since. Obviously, it had meaning for her. I found it spooky.

What strikes me now about having stylized pictures of Jesus and crucifixes almost constantly in view at home was that the hideousness of crucifixion had never entered my mind. On Saturday mornings until I was nine or ten, I would go into my parents' room and we'd sit in bed together in our pajamas and play "I spy with my little eye" until it was time to listen to "Big Jon and Sparkie" on the radio. ("It's Saturday, and there's no school today!," the announcer declared, followed by a rendition of "The Teddy Bears' Picnic." The comedic program was sort of like *The Rocky and Bullwinkle Show,* but without the irony) One day just before or after the program, a newscaster related that a murderer had been executed the night before and his last words as he was being strapped to the electric chair were now repeated. In view of the terrible implement of death for my Savior, it is perhaps surprising that my feelings of sympathy were not for Him but for what had happened to the man the night before. The moment passed without my mentioning my feelings then or later, but my dreams for the next months were filled with execution scenarios in which I was about to be electrocuted for unspecified crimes. The agony of the cross, however, which was recalled every day in prayers and whenever I glanced at the walls, was not a reminder of immediate pain, but, rather, just an element of a larger story. In the 1960s, the comedian Dick Gregory created an uproar when he said that if Jesus came back today, He'd be electrocuted and Christians would wear electric chairs around their necks. The same sort of people who cry sacrilege at Gregory's observation do not seem more rightfully outraged by crucifixes made of gold and jewels as fashion statements, to me the real sacrilege.

B y 1954, the St. Alban's congregation had more than doubled and had outgrown the modest church, which held only a hundred people. That building, originally the parish hall for a church named St. John's that was built in a nearby town in 1895, was moved to the present site in the 1940s, when El Cajon began to grow, and was renamed St. Alban's. Along with the building came parts of the old church: the altar, the credence table (which holds the cruets of water and wine and the silver box of unconsecrated wafers), and the communion rail, the latter hand-carved in the 1920s by a rector whose nickname was "Termite" because of his love of woodworking. A parish hall about the size of the church, with a kitchen for parish suppers and after-church coffee hours, was attached shortly before my father arrived. The building fund for a new church drew remarkably generous support and a local bank offered a thirty-year mortgage for the remainder. (It was paid off in ten and there was a great celebration in the parish hall, during which the mortgage papers were burned.) A member of the congregation was an architect, who offered his services for nothing, and much of the work on the building, from digging the foundation to doing the framing and laying the floor to hammering together the roof and walls, was done by parishioners who brought their tools every Tuesday afternoon and Saturday and accomplished the work within two years. Those who couldn't do carpentry cooked meals. There were cans of beer at the end of work, and it was one of those that my father imbedded in the foundation.

The new church had an A-frame roof that rose to more

than thirty feet and gave the nave and sanctuary an airy look. Where the old church had a dark, heavy interior, this one was light. The pews, which could seat about three hundred people, were of butterscotch oak, the walls white, the carpet red. Copper and opaque glass light fixtures hung on long chains from the ceiling. A loft above the narthex (the entry area from the street) held the organ and choir. Stained-glass windows, one of Saint John, given by the parish in honor of my father, let in colorful light. The altar from the old church was put in a small chapel on the right side of the nave. To the right of the chancel was the sacristy, where the priest and acolytes robed. Across from it was a room for the altar guild, the group of volunteer women (always women then) who set up the vessels for the service and arranged flowers for the altar. To the left of the chancel was my father's office, its outside door about thirty feet from the rectory.

The church was an extension of our house, and was as comfortable to be in. Our house was an extension of the church, as well, and our lives were ordered around it. Thursday nights I often helped my father, an avid amateur printer, set the type, reverse letter by reverse letter, for the Sunday bulletins in a small room in the parish hall that he had turned into a printing shop. In time I was able to rhythmically pull out the printed sheet as the press opened and slide in a clean one before it closed at a speed almost as fast as his. He had bought the old roller press driven by a large flywheel for a hundred dollars and was happy for any excuse to use it—for the parish stationary, our annual Christmas cards, and such odds and ends as three-by-five cards with the St. Alban's emblem and the injuction "Drive

The frame of the new church
next to the rectory, 1955

Prayerfully" in bright red ink. In the days before Palm Sunday, my parents and I folded and wove together hundreds of palm crosses. We always made more than would be needed, so the remainder could be burned and used on the next year's Ash Wednesday, when my father would dip his right thumb into the ashes and make the sign of the cross on parishioners' foreheads as a reminder of mortality, and say, "Remember, O man, that dust thou art and unto dust shalt thou return." We opened Christmas presents at 1:30 a.m., after the midnight service on Christmas Eve—which filled the church to overflowing—because there was another service on Christmas morning. (One of my presents was being allowed to sleep in.) The first item of business after we returned home was for me to find a parishioner's annual gift of a bottle of King's Ransom scotch. Even wrapped, the squat rectangular box was easy to spot under the tree, and I poured my father his usual drink of one and one-half ounces of liquor and three ounces of water, which, after a first good swig, he would nurse until we went to bed. Then we set to work on the other presents. Despite the rigors of the just-completed long service, my father was always in a playful mood.

"You know, when I was growing up in Elsecar," he said one time, "we didn't have a lot of money. Our Christmas present was often a fresh orange. One year things were particularly tough at the mine and my father couldn't afford a nice tree, but he did get a good deal on one that had no greenery. He was worrying about how it could be made festive when, on the way home, he found a shiny brass bullet in the street that he picked up to use as a bright decoration." He paused as his dark eyes twinkled. "That was the year we had a cartridge in a bare tree."

Despite his lightheartedness, my father was serious about his faith. He held a very orthodox theology regarding the Articles of Faith spelled out in the Episcopal prayer book and his thoroughly outlined course for interested parishioners on the teaching of the Church was quite specific: "Religion is revealed as man can assimilate it. . . . Man began on a higher plane and has degenerated . . . he is not evolving from savage to civilized but back to a higher life. . . . Christian teaching begins with a man made in God's image who fell. . . . Faith means an attitude of life, covering will, instinct, feeling, and reason. . . . Christian doctrine is actually organized thinking about God." And so on. But he was not lockstep in his faith. Every year he would test his belief by reading the work of a literate agnostic. He opened his mind to George Bernard Shaw and Bertrand Russell—and Mickey Spillane, too—to try to see if he had missed something or if he were kidding himself. (He kept the Spillane out of sight, on the top shelf of a kitchen cabinet, as if it were a guilty pleasure that would corrupt my mother and me.) He told me that nothing he read ever dissuaded him, but there came a time in the mid-1950s when he did consider giving up the priesthood, the result not of words or ideas but, rather, of a lowly fungus that left his hands with open sores and made them red and swollen. It was probably a contact dermatitis or food allergy that could be more readily identified today, but at the time, no treatment worked. For a priest such as my father, not being able to use his hands threatened his ability to do much of his pastoral care—giving Communion, baptizing babies, laying his hands on and praying for the sick, even giving a simple blessing. He wore white gloves during church, soaked his hands in foul mixtures prepared by apothecaries, solutions that turned them a deep chestnut red; he dried them with towels, let them dry in the sun and in the shade. No difference. This went on for three or four months. He later told me that he and my mother talked seriously and often about whether he could continue and remain effective. And then, almost as suddenly as the affliction came, it disappeared. In my later life I've often wondered whether there was a more psychological cause for the lengthy infection, if it happened during a period when he challenged his faith and this time did not have an immediate rebuttal.

Throughout this time, my father kept his sense of humor, and throughout his life, he loved telling jokes, which had an extra edge because of his English accent and sense of language. He had fast comic reflexes that produced funny puns and asides, and great timing in the delivery of long shaggy-dog stories—he could drag one out for minutes—and short groaners.

"Did you hear about the cannibal who passed his brother in the jungle?" he asked me, all innocence, one night as he and my mother and I ate dinner. She appreciated his humor, though occasionally she would roll her eyes or say, "Oh, *Jack!*" She also left the joke telling to him. Her light remarks had a stiff-upper-lip quality honed by the Depression. When something went wrong she'd say, "If it's not one thing, it's six" or "Worse things happen at sea."

St. Andrew's School went only through fourth grade, and as there was not another parochial elementary school anywhere nearby, when I finished, I enrolled in the public school in El Cajon. As I approached graduation from eighth grade, my greatest ambition in life was to go to El Cajon High ("Home of the Braves") and wear a red Braves jacket to school every day. My parents had other ideas. Several wealthy Episcopalians in and around the San Diego suburbs of National City and Chula Vista had recently founded San Miguel School for Boys, with classes for grades seven through twelve, and my parents enrolled me for the ninth grade. I was bereft. I liked church well enough, but the idea of going to a church school with a hundred boys spread through six grades was a little much. No Braves jacket. No Friday-night football games under the lights. No low-rider car. No girls.

The school building was a well-worn Victorian mansion in National City, fifteen miles away, and to my surprise, I quickly came to like it. The day began with Morning Prayer; there was Holy Communion on Fridays. My ninth-grade English teacher, who incessantly made us diagram sentences to learn the parts of speech and their relationship to one another, obviously had his mind on things other than the service one of those Fridays, because as soon as we sat down in his class, he wrote the opening of the Prayer of Consecration on the blackboard:

All glory be to thee, Almighty God, our heavenly Father, for that thou, of thy tender mercy, didst give thine only Son Jesus Christ to suffer death upon the Cross for our redemption; who made there (by his one oblation of himself once offered) a full, perfect, and sufficient sacrifice, oblation, and satisfaction, for the sins of the whole world; and did institute, and in his holy Gospel command us to continue, a perpetual memory of that his precious death and sacrifice, until his coming again. . . .

Then he said with a sadistic grin, "Diagram it."

Along with the regular array of high school courses, San Miguel also required that students take Sacred Studies. For one class in my junior year, we had to write a paper on part of Exodus 3, in which God calls to Moses from the burning bush and instructs him to lead the Israelites out of Egypt. When Moses, still reeling from the encounter and what he is being asked to do, says, "Behold, when I come unto the children of Israel, and shall say unto them, The God of your fathers hath sent me unto you; and they shall say to me, What is his name? what shall I say unto them? And God said unto Moses, I AM THAT I AM: and he said, Thus shalt thou say unto the children of Israel, I AM hath sent me unto you."

I struggled with the meaning of all this. I failed to understand that God was in effect saying, "I am *because* I am," that He was before all things, that no one created Him. More important, I failed to take the assignment seriously. I was working at the dining room table that night and my father stopped by to see what I was writing. I showed him the passage and he asked me what I thought it meant. I replied cavalierly, "It looks like God is blowing His own horn."

There were only a few times in my childhood that I made my father furious; this was one of them. He made it abundantly clear that my lack of respect for God would not be tolerated.

For the most part, however, I was devout, if unquestioning. I thought non-Episcopalians were misguided or unenlightened. I thought Jews—well, I didn't think much about Jews. They were Old Testament people and I didn't know any. When in ninth grade I first heard an anti-Semitic remark from an upper classman, I thought it funny rather than repellant.

Besides Camp Stevens, and probably because of it, I was

active in the Episcopal Young Churchmen on the diocesan level. I was a regular member and often an officer of the St. Alban's youth group and over the years at camp I met hundreds of kids from churches all over the Diocese of Los Angeles, which at the time extended from near Santa Barbara, ninety miles north of Los Angeles, to San Diego and the towns along the Mexican border, 125 miles to the south. My junior year of high school, I was vice president of the EYC and in the spring before my senior year I was elected president. A few days later I received a telegram from a priest I liked a lot who was often at camp. It simply said, "Congratulations. Collect Trinity 19." I didn't have to look in the prayer book. The collect (said before the reading of the Epistle and always one sentence) for the nineteenth Sunday after Trinity is commonly used as an all-purpose prayer: "O God, forasmuch as without thee we are not able to please thee; Mercifully grant that thy Holy Spirit may in all things direct and rule our hearts; through Jesus Christ our Lord."

In that summer of 1961, the new vice president and I, along with the two priests who were in charge of diocesan youth activities, drove to Ann Arbor, Michigan, for a national convocation of Episcopal Young Churchmen and young people from several branches of Protestantism. The priests, perhaps in their forties, were a hoot. We traded stints at the wheel and one taught me how to draft behind a car before pulling around to pass, thus doing it in the shortest space. We told jokes and sang songs. A steak dinner in Omaha still lingers in memory.

We stayed in dorm rooms at the University of Michigan, where the convocation was held. It was meant to be

an exercise in ecumenicity, and it worked. The highlight
for me was a service where we gathered to hear "A New
American Folk Mass," which set the psalms and other sung
parts of the service to modern music. I found it extraordi-
narily entertaining and moving. A service had never felt so
alive to me and, it seemed, to almost everyone there. I
bought a recording of it and played it for my parents, who,
somewhat to my surprise, loved it as well.

When it came time to apply to colleges, I had little idea
of what to do. I was a champion swimmer in our local
league, but despite a couple of tryouts at Southern California colleges, I was not going to get a swimming scholarship.
Because I loved the water and spent every spare moment I
had bodysurfing, I would have been happy to go to San
Diego State, join a fraternity, and surf through life. It was
my second English teacher who not only led me to understand the pleasure of writing but who also took me aside
one day and said, "Lax, if you stay in California, you'll end
up a beach bum. You need to go east." He had attended
Hobart College in Geneva, New York, after World War II
and suggested I apply there. It was affiliated with the Episcopal Church and offered clergy scholarships. As my father
was making about seven thousand dollars a year, I'd need
one. I applied. Shortly thereafter, in a stroke of beneficial
coincidence, my father met the bishop of the Diocese of
Western New York, Lauriston L. Scaife, who was visiting
San Diego in the hope of persuading my father's good
friend the Reverend Harold Robinson to go to Buffalo as
dean of the Cathedral. Harold and my father were at a
clergy conference at Harold's church, the largest in our
part of the diocese, and the bishop invited my father to join

them. The subject of children came up and the bishop asked where I was applying to college. When my father mentioned Hobart, the bishop said, "I'm on the board; I want to meet this young man." I was pulled from a class at San Miguel to go to the phone.

"Wash your face and get down to St. Paul's right away," my father said. "The bishop of Western New York wants to meet you."

My career as a beach bum was over before it could begin. Undoubtedly because of the bishop, and perhaps also because I was a rare applicant from California, Hobart accepted me and gave me a four-hundred-dollar clergy scholarship, along with a job in the kitchen to cover my meals. With my earning what it cost for my books and spending money, we covered the $2,200 yearly cost.

Before I left for college, my father took me aside, as I expected he would, but gave me unexpected advice. "Son," he said, putting a hand on my shoulder, "if a strange woman comes up to you on a street and offers to take your watch around the corner to have it engraved, don't do it."

With those words to live by, I entered Hobart in September 1962 and, along with other classes, began the two-year required course in Western civilization. For the first time, I understood that the Bible is literature, whether or not it is divine directive. I not only met Jews; I quickly had a circle of Jewish friends who took me to temple. I was stunned to realize that what Rabbi Hillel said before the birth of Christ ("What is hateful to you do not do to your neighbor. That is the whole Torah. The rest is commentary") is mirrored in the Episcopal liturgy: "Hear what our

Lord Jesus Christ saith. Thou shalt love the Lord thy God with all thy heart, and with all thy soul, and with all thy mind. This is the first and great commandment. And the second is like unto it; Thou shalt love thy neighbor as thyself. On these two commandments hang all the Law and the Prophets." Who knew? Between studying the Old and New Testaments, there were the writings of Saints Augustine and Anselm and Thomas Aquinas, and I began to see my faith in a new and more complex light.

Four

Until I entered college, my faith was simple, sincere, and unexamined. Then on the first day of Western civ, I opened my syllabus and there on the front page was Socrates' famous (though not yet to me) dictum, "The unexamined life is not worth living." My classmates and I were directed to make life worth living through lectures Tuesdays and Thursdays, exams on Saturdays, and small group discussions in between that took on the ages-old Really Big Questions, which an education in the humanities tries to answer: What is the human situation? What is the nature of the universe? What is man's place in it? Why are we here? How should we behave? Starting with "the Hebrew, as compared with Mesopotamian and Egyptian, myths of origin," we learned about the formation of the people of Israel, the conquest of Canaan and tribal confederation, Hebrew monarchy and the beginnings of prophecy, the era of Jeremiah and the fall of Jerusalem, the prophets of the exile, and the return and rise of Judaism. We closely read Genesis, Joshua, Judges, Samuel, Kings I and II, Amos, Hosea, Isaiah I and II, Jeremiah, Deuteronomy, Ezekiel, Daniel, and Job. We discovered that between 1200 B.C., when the great Babylonian, Hittite, and Egyptian empires declined, and 800 B.C., when the Assyrian Empire rose, many small states emerged in the Near East, but one mattered most so far as our culture is concerned: Without Jews, not much Western civilization. One wit coined a cheer: "All the way with Yahweh!"

Of course, the theme of what we learned is that humankind—starting with Adam and Eve—did *not* go all the way with Yahweh but instead wanted knowledge of good and evil on their own. According to the Old Testament, this sin ultimately led to the destruction of all people save for Noah and his family, though Noah's descendants proved not to have learned anything, as they trusted in themselves to reach heaven via the Tower of Babel rather than through Yahweh's power. Yahweh tried with one family yet again, this time Abraham's, with more success. Abraham's descendants—the twelve families descended from Jacob's twelve sons—became the chosen. What made the Jews special was both the preservation of their tribal forms for a longer period than in any other patriarchal society and that their tribal association was anchored to a unique covenant relationship with their God. Yahweh confirmed this covenant through Moses, then fulfilled His part of the deal by delivering the twelve tribes from Egypt and giving them dominion in Canaan, a hegemony that reached its apogee in the reign of King David.

This basic story stays in many parts the same over eight hundred years but is refined, reinterpreted, and given greater significance in four stages: first by the eighth-century B.C. prophets Amos, Hosea, Micah, and Isaiah; then by the seventh- and sixth-century B.C. prophets of crisis and captivity, Jeremiah, Ezekiel, Second Isaiah, and the Deuteronomists; third, around 400 B.C., by the priests of Ezra's time; and finally and most radically by the writers of the New Testament.

Not that this was necessarily historical fact, we learned. Similarities to various parts of the story exist in Babylonian, Accadian, and Egyptian legends, for instance. But fact and faith are quite clearly two different things, and the point of the supposed facts that compose the story are meant to lead us to understand God's relation to mankind and to worship Him through our faith. In the Bible, God is not a local power who lives, say, in a river or in a volcano. What these stories lead to as they are refined through the New Testament is that ours is a God who is not confined by one place, but a single, omnipotent God who transcends all. Remember the First Commandment.

Added to this fluidity is the problem of translation. Christianity began as a sect of Judaism and it took about a generation after the Crucifixion to become an almost exclusively Gentile religion popular in the eastern part of the Roman Empire, which meant that it was adopted primarily by Greek-speaking people. (Look to whom Saint Paul wrote many of his epistles: Corinthians, Galatians,

Thessalonians, Ephesians, Philippians.) Though later it would attract Latin speakers (the Epistle to the Romans), even as Christianity's popularity grew in the West, the Church was predominately Greek-speaking until the end of the second century. Thus Hebraic notions and accounts had to be translated into a Greek context, and later into a Latin one. (American English speakers often have a narrower view of Christ's teachings. Though the story is probably apocryphal, there is validity to the notion. "English was good enough for Jesus Christ and it's good enough for the children of Texas," Texas governor Miriam "Ma" Ferguson supposedly said in 1924.)

This wasn't exactly what I had learned in Sunday school, which was tilted mightily toward the New Testament, a series of supposed divinely inspired documents that sought to tell the life and acts of Jesus over the thirty-three years of His life rather than through hundreds of years of Hebraic history of the Old Testament. In my life until then, Christianity was a cohesive, linear story. Now I had an entirely different way of thinking about God, and it led to hours of late-night dorm conversations that grew even more animated when the second semester rolled around and we came to Jesus, the early Church, Saint Paul, the confrontation of Christianity and the Greek mind, the Church and the Roman Empire, Saint Augustine and the fall of the West. The Book of Common Prayer, where I had been content to find my answers, was suddenly a slim volume indeed. But, perhaps strangely, the intellectual free-for-all of the classroom discussions and nightly reading were held in a part of my mind separate from where faith resided. Church remained an easy comfort; I left what I was learning in the classroom at the chapel door.

I continued as an acolyte in the college chapel on Sundays and went at least once a week for Evening Prayer. I had then an unshakable sense of partnership with God and felt completely confident that I was being watched out for, as if He had my calling card and knew my name. One spring evening I sat on the quad with a friend whose father was a priest and recounted my experience of sliding headlong toward the rim of the Grand Canyon and being sure that God had saved me from slipping farther. It was a story I had told only once or twice before and I had a deep sense of safety as I recalled it with a goofy smile. A few years later, a new friend told me of her recent conversion to Christianity and her own sense of safety. I smiled knowingly and said, "Welcome to the fellowship of the silly grin."

With the backing of such certainty I immersed myself in Plato and Saint Augustine, in abstract idealism, and, as Saint John put it toward the beginning of his Gospel, the Word made flesh. Plato argued that *Logos,* the Word, the rational ideal, could not be made concrete and could be seen only in the shadow of the cave and was thus an abstraction. But Augustine, four hundred years after Christ, argued that what made Christianity the answer was that Christians believed the Church to be the Body of Christ, and therefore the living embodiment of reason. "And the Word was made flesh and dwelt among us," John 1:14 goes, "(and we beheld his glory, the glory as of the only begotten of the Father,) full of grace and truth."

A central theme of all this reading and study was a continuation of the intellectual and spiritual challenge to prove God's omnipotence, what we saw in the resolution of the Old Testament. Augustine began writing *The City of God* three years after the fall of Rome in 410 as a rebuttal to the pagan notion that Rome was susceptible to being conquered because, in accepting Christianity as the official religion of the empire, Rome had abandoned the pagan gods who had protected it. (It was a long rebuttal: It took Augustine thirteen years to finish *De Civitate Dei*.) He postulates the perfect city of God and the imperfect city of man, formed by opposite kinds of love: the earthly by the love of self, even to the contempt of God; and the city of God by the love of God, even to the sacrifice of self. For Augustine, love and will are the same. Perhaps the best-known story about Augustine is his account in Book 2 of his *Confessions* of stealing pears with a group of friends. The story itself is a simple case of youthful hubris and minor juvenile delinquency. Augustine didn't even want the pears—he tossed them to pigs—but the thrill of illicit behavior, of doing something wrong because he *could,* allowed him to assume power over God in the breaking of His laws. But, he argues, that very act of imitation proves God's omnipotence. The story is really a metaphor for the quest for understanding and proof of God's supremacy. It is another version of Adam and Eve, of man's vain attempt to be God-like and stumbling badly in the process. For a popular version of this, think of "The Sorcerer's Apprentice" in *Fantasia,* where the apprentice, believing he can be sorcerer-like and command a broom to do his menial job of hauling buckets of water from a well, instead commands the broom to multiply again and again and produce an unstoppable flood until the sorceror breaks the spell. The message is the same: We cannot act safely without a higher power to guide us.

I had never spent much, if any, time trying to prove the existence of God. Now much of my days and nights were spent learning how the greatest divines and philosophers did so. In the eleventh century, 650 years after Augustine, Saint Anselm of Canterbury wrote about *fides quaerens intellectum*—faith seeking understanding. By this he meant not to replace blind faith with reasoned understanding but, rather, to augment a love of God with a deeper understanding of God.

Anselm's were the first definitions of God and of faith that made me stop and think. Anselm claims the proof of God's existence is that God is something "than which nothing greater can be conceived," and it continues as a syllogism: If that than which nothing greater can be conceived can be conceived in the mind, it must exist in reality. Thus that than nothing greater can be conceived exists in reality. And so God exists.

Finally, insofar as my reliance on saints for instruction went, Thomas Aquinas takes an even simpler route to the primacy of God in his *Summa Theologica* (1267–1273). Aquinas was a Christian Aristotelian: The universe is definable and ordered, he says, with all things placed on a metaphorical ladder that eventually reaches God, the one and only necessity in the universe, its one self-sufficient being. In 1879, Pope Leo XIII declared Aquinas's scholasticism the official philosophy of Catholicism.

My faith to this point in life was traditionally defined:

belief without necessity of proof. God had lived in my heart all my life. Now He was dwelling in my mind, as well. The nights sitting up in the dorm talking about God or arguing over coffee in the student union provided a new vocabulary of faith. I didn't realize it at the time, but this constant intellectual pursuit of God grew to be a second leg for my faith to stand on. Or so it seemed.

Advice was something my father seldom gave, and this was noticeable in a clergyman. There were his parting words when I left for college, and there was an instance when we both were at Camp Stevens the summer after my freshman year and he gave me a lesson in anger management. I had received an irate letter from the mother of an on-and-off-again long-distance girlfriend, chastising me for what she called the "gobbledygook" I was giving her daughter about our relationship. I immediately wrote my own irate response. I showed it, along with the mother's letter, to my father, who knew her and her husband, another priest in the diocese.

"I understand how you feel," he told me. "But maybe you should do what I do when something like this happens, which is read the letter tomorrow and then decide whether to send it."

"All right," I said, still full of righteous indignation, "but I know I'll send it then."

The next day I reread my letter and ripped it up.

Otherwise, there were very few pieces of counsel he offered. In retrospect it may be that he didn't need to give a lot of advice, as he conducted himself in a way that was advisory to anyone who paid attention.

Faith, Interrupted

Spending all that time in my sophomore year studying many theologians whose purpose was either to prove the existence of God or examine His nature led me to spend much time in personal thought about this. I had talked with my father some about Augustine, Anselm, and Aquinas, but he was not one for trying to count the angels dancing on the head of a pin, and sometimes he just used aspects of religion for our mutual amusement.

"My dear, dear son," he wrote one day,

> Dealing with the fascinating subject of "Occuli
> Episcopi," or "the Eyes of Bishops," is most aptly set
> out in a rather tendentious work of the noted writer
> and apologist, The Rev. Dr. Crozier, who, writing
> under the pseudonym of "The Crook," points
> out that bishops first rose to fame in Italy and
> France, and therefore, whatever means are used to
> measure the "Occuli Episcopi" must agree with both
> countries in time and terrain. As this fame reached
> its peak in the Medieval period, it is obvious that the
> only common denominator which could fulfill all
> demands is the metric system, and, using this as a
> standard, he arrives at the startling, but completely
> logical, conclusion that bishops are shortsighted
> and inordinately fond of tripe. To prove his point,
> he notes that almost all bishops of this period
> were portrayed by noted artists, and that they
> invariably have a buxom wench in close proximity,
> and therefore short- (or near-) sightedness was a
> definite asset. Indeed, if the good doctor is to be
> believed, it was during this period that the now

famous ecclesiastical expression "bosom friends" gained prominence.

As tripe is a product of the mammary glands of our beefy (or buxom) bovine friends, he counts his theory well proven that "Occuli Episcopi" means "shortsighted and fond of tripe," and goes on to prove in his "Quod erat demonstrandum" that the pendulum swings both ways only when it is in motion, that infinity always meets itself coming back, and rarely does the Apostolic See.

It may well be that you do not agree with him, in which case I can only suggest that you read "The Frustration of Futility" by N. E. Priest, and "The Trident," or "The Three Horns of a Dilemma Concerning the Trinity," written by a West Coast divine whose name for the moment escapes me.

This letter, for all its joking, gives a glimpse into my father's thinking about the priesthood—the frustrations, the constant challenge to goodness in a difficult world, the din that can drown out the voice of God.

My sophomore year brought other personal foment beside the whether or not of God's existence—I performed one of my two real acts of conscience in college. The Episcopal Church was an early advocate for civil rights (early, at least in terms of the 1950s and 1960s, though one might well ask where they or any group of white Christians were before that), and my father and I were drawn to the movement, which influenced my thinking and behavior. Through my college years, the civil rights movement continued to gain momentum, though there was monstrosity along with promise. The soaring possibility of the August 1963 march on Washington, where Martin Luther King, Jr., gave his "I have a dream" speech, was shattered eighteen days later by the bombing of the Sixteenth Street Baptist Church in Birmingham, Alabama, and the deaths of four young girls in the explosion. But in July 1964, Congress passed the Civil Rights Act, and in December Dr. King took the Southern Christian Leadership Conference to Selma, Alabama, to join in the Alabama Right to Vote Project, which had been under way for over a year. The marches from Selma to the capital of Montgomery began in March 1965. Dr. King called for white clergy to come in support and many did, including some from the Diocese of Los Angeles.

My father was an ardent supporter of King, and any vestiges of his "White Man's burden" outlook were now gone, as evidenced by the troubles with our doctor friend that were reaching their own crescendo. Yet my father's and my own support for racial equality were more in principal than practice because the truth is, neither of us knew many black people. There were a few black priests in our diocese, but their parishes were in Los Angeles, and my father saw most of them only at the yearly diocesan clergy conference. Until I met a couple of them and their sons and a few others in their congregations at Camp Stevens in my early teens, my sole experience with a black kid was when one enrolled at Cajon Valley Junior High School in

1955, when I was in seventh grade. A day or two later, someone put a sign saying W H I T E S   O N L Y over one of the drinking fountains, and racial slurs were etched on another wall. The boy withdrew from school before I even met him. I recall no repercussions, no assembly where the principal upbraided intolerance. The black student was there, then he wasn't, and we went on.

One of the clergy who answered Dr. King's call to come to Selma was the Reverend James Reeb, a thirty-eight-year-old Unitarian minister in Boston who was scorned and taunted by racist white onlookers, as were the other white clergy who went. As Reeb and two fellow ministers walked to get dinner—in a "colored" restaurant, because no white place would serve them—a band of whites closed in behind them, calling them niggers. Reeb's companions moved quickly ahead, but he kept his steady pace. Moments later, one of his companions turned to see where he was, just as Reeb was clubbed on the head. His skull was crushed, and he died the next day.

"My dear faint hope of a future America," my father wrote two days after the murder.

> The situation in Alabamy is something, isn't it?
> Makes you wonder whether we have really
> progressed at all. The Bishop sent telegrams last
> Monday and we are doing what we can here, but
> how can you fight blind prejudice? The Bishop sent
> one layman and three clergy to Selma but I have not
> heard their report yet. There is to be a memorial
> service in Balboa Bowl for Reeb tomorrow, attended
> by most churches. I am proud of our Bishop. More

and more he has taken a stand against these things.
More and more I am convinced that our churches
are resorts for a lot of country club Xns. [Christians]
who want to be respectable, and who have no idea
what the Xn. religion is all about, but I am also
convinced that there are more people trying to live
up to Xn. principles within the Church than there
are nominal Xns. In short, I have hopes for the
Church . . . even with me in it.

And so, my first act of conscience. At the start of my
sophomore year, I had pledged a fraternity. It had a cross
section of students: blacks, whites, Christians, Jews, ath-
letes, scholars. It threw great parties as well, and for a
nineteen-year-old with no car in an upstate New York
town with little nightlife, fraternities had special appeal.
The state's drinking age at that time was eighteen, so parties had kegs of beer, punches made from unhealthy combinations of multiple spirits, and live bands. I got to church
most Sunday mornings, but not always with a clear head.

The motto of the fraternity was a quote from the
Roman emperor Constantine, who in 312 prayed for
divine assistance before the battle of Milvian Bridge
against his coemperor and brother-in-law, Maxentius. In
the midday light, Constantine saw a cross inscribed *in hoc
signo vinces*—"by this sign you will conquer." In a dream
that night, God told Constantine to use the sign of the
cross in all his battles. He converted to Christianity and
made it the official religion of the empire. Every pledge
had to learn the motto, along with a lot of silly things that
constituted our verbal hazing.

Around the time early in the fall semester that I pledged the fraternity, I came to know a junior who the previous year had worked for the Episcopal Church on college campuses. He was a member of the fraternity but did not seem to spend any time at the house. One day while we were talking about his work for the Church, the conversation expanded and he asked me what I thought of the fraternity motto. I said that I found it quaint but hadn't given it much thought. He told me that while our chapter was wonderfully inclusive, the national charter excluded Jews and blacks. I was astonished that a member was required to be a "bona fide white male student." (This was not rescinded until 1970.) His questions regarding my feelings about prejudice and exclusion got me thinking about whether to stay a member and what kind of statement it would make if I withdrew. After some thought, I resigned. Doing so had more to do with my heightened sense of civil rights and discrimination than with my faith. Certainly it was something of an odd choice, because our chapter was an example of what the fraternity could be everywhere and there was a good argument for making changes from within, but I just couldn't square that with my feelings about the national organization.

My resignation caused no stir. The brothers acknowledged the anomaly and said they felt they were striking a blow for equality by going on as they were. While my decision was momentous to me as an act of principle, my principles didn't stop me from accepting an open invitation to all future parties. (In a bit of irony, beside my graduation picture in the yearbook, I'm listed as a member.)

"I am just a wee bit proud that you are not joining because you do not agree with the philosophy behind the fraternity," my father wrote to me. "Fatherly advice: never do anything against your principles unless it will do some good. End of fatherly advice. By 'unless it will do some good' I mean that I am opposed to breaking up a marriage, but sometimes when there is continual drunkenness, or cruelty, or faithlessness, I must advise a separation even though it goes against my principles."

So not only is the unexamined life not worth living, the principled life cannot be lived without compromise.

Along with my enthusiasm for racial equality came an intrigue with Dr. King's philosophy of nonviolence and, like King, I turned to Mohandas Gandhi for more instruction.

On January 20, 1965, in the middle of my junior year, Lyndon B. Johnson said in his presidential inaugural address that America "can never again stand aside, prideful in isolation. Terrific dangers and troubles that we once called 'foreign' now constantly live among us." In February, following an attack by Vietcong guerrillas on the U.S. military compound at Pleiku, Johnson ordered the bombing of a North Vietnamese army camp. Opinion polls showed an 80 percent approval of the bombing and a 70 percent approval for Johnson, and he agreed to his advisers' long-standing recommendation to begin sustained bombing of North Vietnam. (By the end of the war, U.S. military planes would have flown three million sorties and dropped eight million tons of bombs, more than four times the amount in World War II, leading to three million civilian refugees and hundreds of thousands of deaths.)

In April, fifteen thousand students demonstrated against the war. Around that time the upperclassman whose questioning had led me to withdraw from the fraternity and I had hours of conversation about the war while we walked, drank coffee, or sat under the stars on the quad. He pressed me on my feelings about the war, about whether it was justified, about killing, about an individual's responsibility for his beliefs. I found it hard to justify the war and harder to justify the continual bombing. I told him that on account of how I perceived Jesus to have lived His life and what He preached, I believed it was wrong to kill. After listening to my answers, he asked if I was a conscientious objector to war. I hadn't thought much about that. All my life, I had abhorred harsh verbal arguments, avoided fist-fights, and was considered a peacemaker by my friends. But no one in my extended family found war in conflict with their religious training and belief, and my feelings about going to war were not something I had ever had to truly consider before now. Maybe so, I told him. Others on campus were also considering whether they were COs, and I talked with a few I knew.

I didn't speak much about this to anyone else as I sorted through it in my mind. I went to the Book of Common Prayer and the Bible for guidance, making sure of what I thought was in there. I considered the difference between nonviolence and pacifism.

In July 1965, President Johnson announced that he would send forty-four combat battalions to Vietnam, rais-

ing the total number of American soldiers there to
125,000.

"I have asked the commanding general, General Westmoreland, what more he needs to meet this mounting
aggression," the president said. "He has told me. And we
will meet his needs. We cannot be defeated by force of
arms. We will stand in Vietnam."

The number of draftees was doubled, to 35,000 a
month.

"I do not find it easy to send the flower of our youth, our
finest young men, into battle," Johnson continued. "I have
spoken to you today of the divisions and the forces and the
battalions and the units, but I know them all, every one. I
have seen them in a thousand streets, of a hundred towns,
in every state in this union—working and laughing and
building, and filled with hope and life. I think that I know,
too, how their mothers weep and how their families sorrow. This is the most agonizing and the most painful duty
of your President."

As one of the petals on the "the flower of our youth"
who could feel the wilting breath of his local draft-board
members on his neck, the question of whether I was a
conscientious objector was now real rather than philo-
sophical. I had a student deferment through college. After
that, I would be reclassified.

One of my classmates and fellow acolytes at St.
John's Chapel was George Packard, known as
"Skip." He was from Wantagh, Long Island,
twenty miles from Manhattan. Even as a sophomore, he
was already one of the big men on campus. Tall and ath-

letic, a member of the lacrosse team, he was one of those people who seem natural leaders. In another person, the success he had on campus might not have come so easily, because what grounded him was not necessarily what most people in the 1960s would consider cool. He was a regular at his parish's services, a devoted Episcopalian, having come to the Church by marital compromise: Before his parents' wedding, his mother was a Roman Catholic and his father, a marketing consultant, belonged to the United Church of Christ. Skip's father was in many ways a model of loyal and devoted service: He was active in his parish and a member of the vestry, and he was also much involved in civic affairs and with the Boy Scouts. It was he who kept the family attending services; like all kids, Skip had no say in the matter. He was not baptized until he was five. (His one memory of the event is his dropping his water gun and it skittering across the floor.) His parish priest was one of those people who could make the Church come alive to a teenager, and Skip was drawn in. It was he who organized the training for the other acolytes. (He got his nickname immediately after his birth. His father was on duty in the navy when his mother went into labor. Each time the nurse brought in her new son to feed, she'd say, "Here's my little skipper.")

As I followed my father in church, Skip followed his outside it, as a committed Boy Scout; neither choice impressed many at that time. When Skip ran for class office in high school, his campaign manager sought to play down or omit the Scouts and his church activities from his résumé, pointing out that these were more likely to be social hindrances than a help. As Skip later put it, he shrugged at the advice and said he'd take his chances. "It is what it is," he said. "I know these institutions in a different way than how they appear." I suspect that the years of learning self-reliance in wilderness camping and leading other Scouts developed his capacity to draw people to him, and that the unconscious acceptance that comes from being part of a congregation added to his confidence.

"These kinds of organizational events were below the radar," he said to me many years later as we talked about our faith in high school and college. "It was something that was given to us because the people in that environment were not socially accepted in the more rigorous social milieu. The Church creates an acceptance level that you don't realize you're signing on for. The Body of Christ is the Kingdom of God, where every person who draws a breath is there. They're there not because they're worthy, but because they're loved. So the Church and the Holy Spirit kind of works on you like that. In a way it spoils you, because you can't function in that regard in fraternities or in a platoon system or in other social environments by being the meanest son of a bitch possible. There's always going to be this softer edge that's called into play if you've signed on to this other body. I don't think I ever knew this was happening. We're brought there by people who are wiser, smarter, gentler, probably more righteous than we are. My worry is that I've not significantly done this for others, that I've not passed this on to my children."

In the fall of 1965, at the beginning of our senior year, we became roommates by fortuitous happenstance. I was

*Eric (left) and Skip just before
graduation from Hobart, 1966*

the head proctor, or resident assistant, for the dorm. He
was in charge of all proctors and dorms, and because our
spacious room with two single beds, a large area for sitting
and studying, and a private bathroom was the nicest on
campus, he sensibly chose to live there. We got on wonderfully, with a shared sense of humor and as strong a
sense of irony as twenty-one-year-olds can have. He had a
beat-up Volkswagen that he let me use, and which con-
veyed us on a couple of wild, hormone-induced late-night
road trips. I didn't give any thought to his much more
marked sense of order than my own. He carefully separated his socks, underwear, and other clothes in the
bureau and put labels of content on each drawer. I once
rearranged his clothes so that nothing was where it should
be, to my amusement and his dismay. Neither of us knew

he had incipient obsessive-compulsive disorder, at the time not a commonly diagnosed condition.

We often lay in our beds and talked for a few minutes after turning out the lights. Usually the chatter was about girls, but sometimes we turned to faith. In one of those talks, we got on to how he felt about being an acolyte, which he enjoyed. But he added that he did not have the feeling of kinship with God that I had, and he repeated what he said he'd told a high school girlfriend about being an acolyte: "I feel I'm going through a performance up there." His performance, however, did not preclude his sense that we had a lot to learn in matters of faith, and he realized far better than I did that a deeper spiritual life was possible. "I think," he said on another night as we talked about what we believed, "we're average guys skating around on the surface here." (Many years later he reflected on that observation as an instance of "being more intuitive than rational. We dipped into one of those timeless moments that are always trying to break through and touch us.")

Along with being in charge of the dorms, Skip was head of the student government, and he was one of three members of the Druids, the senior honor society. Besides the war, the other great topic on campus was the fight, with Skip among those at the forefront, to guarantee the inalienable right of women to be in men's dorms, and for the women students not to have to sign in at their own dormitories at 11:15 on weeknights, fifteen minutes after the library closed.

By the beginning of our senior year, when finally I became a good student after three years of mediocrity, on most campuses the war in Vietnam was a vital fact of life and I was comforted that my church had a position on conscientious objection. Though not widely known, the Episcopal Church had long agreed that it was permitted. The bishops of the Anglican Communion, the worldwide body that is led by the archbishop of Canterbury and includes the Episcopal Church (as the Anglican Church is called in the United States), had declared in 1930 and again in 1940 and 1958 that "war as a method of settling international disputes is incompatible with the teaching and example of our Lord Jesus Christ." The Episcopal Peace Fellowship had a handbook for conscientious objectors, which I sent away for. Without telling my father that, I asked him if he objected to war on the basis of religious training and belief. He said he didn't. He had lost a brother and a nephew to war but believed both world wars were unavoidably necessary to defend freedom.

As I grew up, the memories of World War II were still fresh and my father—and I—took pleasure in watching NBC's twenty-six-part television series *Victory at Sea,* which played in syndication again and again throughout the 1950s. Drawing on archival film footage shot by the U.S., British, Japanese, or German navies, each episode focused on a particular campaign—the Battle of the North Atlantic, the attack on Pearl Harbor, the Battle of Midway, antisubmarine patrols in the South Atlantic, the Leyte Gulf campaign—and was edited to make the most of the action. The dramatic narration and Richard Rodgers's stirring musical score made even more of it. The good guys never looked better and the music swathed the action in almost mythic majesty. One of my father's—and our family's—

closest friends was a navy chaplain. Also, among the members of my father's congregation was a highly decorated marine general whose exploits in World War II were the stuff of legend. I remember my father marveling one night as we watched *Victory at Sea* that he'd never imagined he would have so great a soldier as a parishioner.

I hadn't yet told him about my pondering being a CO and I didn't now. My parents had always supported my decisions, but this was one I wasn't sure they would accept and I wanted to be certain of what I felt before I risked their reaction. We lived in a conservative part of California, an area that was dependent on the military for much of its economy, from aircraft manufacturing to navy and marine bases, and my parents had many friends connected with the armed services. They were all staunch Republicans, and so had I been until only recently. I wasn't at all sure whether my parents and our family friends would respect my stance or be appalled by it.

I worked through the arguments of a "good" war versus a "bad" war and whether any war was justified. I couldn't answer that because the wars that had been romanticized to me were before my time. Faced with the evil of Hitler, I can't say whether my pacifism would have prevailed, but from a legal point of view, no one can be asked to answer a hypothetical question. Vietnam, however, was right in front of me and nothing about it looked right. I didn't believe in the domino theory—that if Vietnam fell to the Communists, all of Southeast Asia would follow—but being a conscientious objector depended on religious training and belief, not on geopolitical opinion.

What helped drive me to my decision was, perhaps paradoxically, the increasingly widely held sense that this was an awful and stupid war. Unlike young men at the time of World War II, during which students flocked to enlist in the armed forces, virtually everyone I knew spent his time figuring out how not to be drafted. Yet the folly of Vietnam allowed me to see my pacifist feeling in deeper relief. I believed it was wrong to kill under any circumstance, and a war where there was no Hitler made my stance easier to discern: Oddly enough, a crucible of lesser heat hardened my true belief that fighting was against my religious training.

During my childhood, I saw every day in my father and mother's examples what it means to be a moral person. Right and wrong paths had visible signposts in our house. When I left the shelter of home (and I would say that in many ways I had a sheltered childhood) to go to Hobart, I did not find in what I learned and experienced there cause to reject what I had accepted from my earliest days. My faith was not undermined by examining the Bible as literature or cultural commentary, nor did Augustine's, Anselm's, and Aquinas's dissections, philosophizing, and scholarship smother my faith with rationalization. Going to church did not suddenly seem uncool. I found my commitment to object to armed service because of conscience a confirmation and logical extension of what I had always seen and tried to do. One seemed naturally to lead me to the other.

As my senior year rolled on, I, like all my classmates, faced the question of what to do after graduation. Beginning in my junior year, I had

seriously been considering whether to become a priest,
an idea that had been in my thoughts to one degree or
another for several years. I talked about the priesthood
with Lauriston Scaife, the bishop who had been instrumental in my being accepted at Hobart and who had
become a good friend; he offered to write me a recommendation for seminary. I told him that I couldn't see
myself in a parish with potluck suppers on Wednesdays
and coffee hours after services on Sundays, but I had a
strong feeling for service, as I now realize it, that was
similar to my father's on the prairie. As graduation
approached, an English major by default, I was still
unclear if I had a calling, but I knew I wanted to do something that would benefit others.

I took the federal civil service exam required for application to any government agency, including the Peace Corps,
which interested me. A childhood friend two years older
was a volunteer in Colombia and her letters about her work
fascinated me. The Peace Corps suited my desire to be of
help to others, it bore a certain similarity to my father's
time in Saskatchewan, and, as a disclaimer against total
altruism, it provided a deferment from the draft. I wanted
to act on my belief, but I had no interest in being a martyr.

Until this point in life, I had always followed my father's
theological lead. Deciding that I was a conscientious
objector was the first time I acted independently in a matter of faith, and it was daunting. When finally I was secure
in my decision, I wrote to my parents to say I would apply
for CO status. I told them that my belief from all I had
learned in church and through study and prayer was that
killing was wrong. I thought the life of Jesus was an exam-

ple of pacifism and nonviolence (apart from that incident with the money changers in the temple).

My concern that they would be disappointed in me was groundless. My father was surprised but thoughtful in reply. He said he still believed that wars could be justified and killing was sometimes necessary, but he did not rebuke me. Nor did my mother, who shared his views.

"As I hope you know," he responded, "your mother and I have always said that whether or not we agree with you, we'll support you in whatever you do, so long as you've thought it through." And he asked me to tell him more fully what I felt.

"I've wrestled a lot in my mind with whether I'm cloaking convenience or even cowardice with piety," I wrote back. "But here's my answer to that: In John 15:13 it says, 'Greater love hath no man than this, that a man lay down his life for his friends.' That's how I feel. I'm willing to die for my friends, I'm just not willing to kill for them." (Forty years later, I would discover that this quote from John is the epitaph on my namesake's headstone.)

His answer came by return mail. "You've convinced me of your sincerity," he wrote. "I admire your willingness to die for principle but not kill for it. I haven't changed my position, but I'll think more about yours." He did not ask me to reconsider mine.

That spring of 1966, the Selective Service System announced that it would reinstate a three-hour, 150-question standardized exam for deferments, one that had been used from 1951 to 1963 and then dropped. The heightened importance of the test now as opposed to most of the period of its earlier use was due to the deep engagement of U.S. troops in Vietnam and the prospect of many more to be sent. Theoretically, anyone wishing to go to graduate school who scored 80 percent or above on the test would be entitled to a deferment, though a local draft board could deny the classification if it wished. (The way deferments were decided is that you applied for the lowest classification for which you felt eligible. Students were 2-S. Peace Corps volunteers and others in similar service were 2-A. Conscientious objectors were 1-O. 1-A meant you were immediately draftable. This meant I could apply for 2-A status before having to go for the higher-stakes 1 O.)

The test posed a dilemma for me. I was now certain that I would apply for CO status when my student deferment ran out and if I was not given one for the Peace Corps. If I took the test and scored well enough, that could be of help to me. But if on the off chance I, say, got something in my eye during the exam and thus misread or couldn't read the questions, or I simply mistakenly filled in the wrong answer boxes and scored below eighty, my draft board might argue that I was applying for a CO only because I did poorly on the exam. I had to decide whether to take it or not.

For help, I turned to a few friends and finally to the college dean, who in the past year had become a good friend. He did not share my pacifist views, but he did accept that I genuinely held them. We decided that I should write my local draft board to tell them I would file the papers for CO status at the appropriate time and that because I did not want the test results to be an influence either way, I would not take the exam but, rather, would apply for a Peace Corps deferment and go on from there. Whatever the outcome, I would not go to Canada, where I was born and where I could escape conscription. My point was not to dodge the draft but to engage it through its rules and accept the outcome. It was in every sense a matter of principle and faith. If that meant going to prison were my CO application rebuffed and I was drafted, I'd do that. The potential consequences of my stand were now very real to me. Over the next several years, I would have a regularly recurring nightmare about being in prison, of being mistreated and in despair. From time to time, I would ask myself if this really was the course I was committed to or if it was driven by convenience, and the answer was always that I'd rather be locked up than have to shoot someone.

On May 14, 350,000 students took the test and another 650,000 took it on one of three other dates over the next five weeks: The total number of students who took the test, one million, was two-thirds greater than the total number of those who took it between 1951 and 1963. Skip was among those who took it the first day, and his experience reflected precisely why I had decided not to risk something going wrong. He was, he said many years later, "ill-prepared to take the test. I got there late—maybe I had a hangover that day." On top of that, he actually *did* get something in his eye and spent an hour and a half trying with the proctor of the exam to get it out. He ended up leaving one and a half pages of the answer sheets blank. The proctor filed an irregularity report to be sent to his draft board.

The Peace Corps accepted my application and offered me a spot in Costa Rica. The week before their letter arrived, a bug-repellent company had run a very effective television ad about the efficacy of its product, shot, it said on the screen, in Costa Rica. On this basis alone, I declined the offer and asked if there were another assignment. Fortunately, there was—in the first group of volunteers to be sent to the islands of Micronesia, a place I had never before heard of and immediately assumed to be a small loss of memory in the Pacific, though the translation from the Greek *mikros* and *nesos* is "small islands." The cover of the brochure for the program had a picture of an almost naked boy climbing a palm tree laden with coconuts, the ocean in the background. "The Peace Corps Goes to Paradise," it touted in large letters at the top. For someone who was at the beach whenever possible, it looked pretty good. And there were no claims about insect repellent. I signed on.

Before I went to Key West, Florida, for three months of training, Bishop Scaife invited me to join him on a short trip to England, for which I would need a passport. At the passport agency in New York City, I saw that at the bottom of the passport application was a loyalty oath that had to be signed. Among the words were "defend the Constitution of the United States against all enemies, foreign and domestic." I was by now completely committed to being a CO and took everything about it quite seriously. I asked the clerk to define the word *defend,* inquiring whether or not that meant to bear arms. He no doubt had heard this before and, in any case, was not interested in parsing words with someone he more than likely took to be an example of precisely what was wrong with America. I sent our dialogue to my parents:

Him: "It means what it says there."
Me: "Defend by what means?"
"It's written right there."
"No, it's not. How broadly is the term defined?"
"Look, if you don't like it, then write your own statement and send it to the legal department in Washington."
"Listen, I don't want an argument, just a definition."
"It's written there [pointing to the application]. If you don't like it, write to Washington."
"And how long will it take them to answer?"
"A couple of weeks."
"But I'm leaving next week."
"Too bad."

I looked at all the women signing the oath, none of whom would ever be drafted, and signed my name.

The next day my parents told me that the Peace Corps had sent a telegram to El Cajon saying I had best notify my draft board within three days as to my "intentions in Micronesia."

"Thanks," I said, "I will write and say they are purely honorable."

The Peace Corps liked their three-month training programs for would-be volunteers to have verisimilitude, and hot, humid Key West was a suitable simulacrum for Micronesia, then officially known as the United Nations Trust Territory of the Pacific. It was a conglomeration of islands in the Western Pacific, just above the equator, aggregated out of political convenience rather than cultural sense, and divided into six districts: the Mariana Islands, the northernmost grouping; the Marshall Islands; the Eastern Caroline Islands, with two districts, Ponape and Truk; and the Western Caroline Islands, also with two districts, Yap and Palau. These islands are daubed over an area of water the size of the United States. There are more bits of land amid this area than there are visible stars in the night sky, but their total landmass is less than the area of greater Los Angeles and fewer than a hundred islands are inhabited. To go with the then six administrative districts, there are six major languages and dozens of dialects. I was assigned to the group going to Truk, which, in geographic comparison to the United States, put it in Kansas.

The Truk Lagoon, the remnant of a former volcano forty miles across, is the most inhabited part of Truk, with people living on a dozen islands, but there are four other island groups: the Mortlocks, 160 miles to the southeast; the Western Islands, about 150 miles in that direction; Namonuito Atoll, 150 miles northwest; and the Hall Islands, 70 miles to the north. Each has its own distinct and quite different dialect. In all, there were about 26,000 Trukese at the time. In skin tone, Micronesians are darker than Polynesians and lighter than Melanesians, a very pretty nut brown. Micronesia was first a territory of Spain, which ruled it from the early seventeenth century until the end of the Spanish-American War, in 1898. Germany then bought much of the territory, which, in turn, was ceded to Japan after World War I. During the first years of World War II, much of the Japanese naval fleet nestled safely in Truk's naturally protected waters (there are only two large passes through the reef), out of range of enemy ships and aircraft, though eventually American aircraft carriers were able to launch attacks against it and sink a large number of the vessels, which formed artificial reefs and made for good fishing and scuba diving. The United States took possession of the islands and eventually turned them into the United Nations Trust Territory of the Pacific, though it continued as administrator, oxymoronically (and often just moronically) through the Department of the Interior and many of the lesser lights in its Bureau of Indian Affairs. The islands were considered too strategically important from a military perspective ever to let another country govern, though apparently the feeling was there were so many islands that a few less wouldn't matter, as a couple of the Marshall Islands were evaporated by atomic- and hydrogen-bomb tests. The most important of all the islands was Guam, which served as a mid-Pacific base for military aircraft and, in the escalation of the Vietnam War, was the launching ground of around-the-clock bombing sorties by B-52s and the refueling stop for planes ferrying troops to action. (Micronesia is now the Federated States of Micronesia, and in 1986 it became independent under a compact of free association with the United States. Truk is now Chuuk. I've kept the spelling in use at the time I was there.)

About three hundred recent college graduates comprised the first group of Micronesia volunteers. In Key West, we were billeted in the Casa Marina Hotel, a white stucco pile with a red tile roof that once was elegant and now was one step above condemnation by the departments of health and building safety. My roommate was a crisp-talking Yalie who arrived in a perfectly rumpled white linen suit. We all had our tropical fantasies.

"Dear Parents," I wrote soon after arrival, clearly mindful, it is evident, of moral behavior.

> Your errant son, as usual remorseful for his sinful ways, once again will try to inform you of some of all that has happened in hot, humid, tepid-watered Key West.
>
> I am learning a new language, that of the Truk District of Micronesia. The language has a close kept fraternity of 26,000 who speak it and treasure the one existing dictionary, which is almost totally useless. Of the 12 weeks of training, 3 will be spent in camps on one of the smaller keys, 2 in Miami living with Cuban families and teaching in the schools (to acquaint us with living with and teaching people who speak no English) and the rest at the lovely Casa Marina. Our days are very busy with language and cultural training, psychological and linguistic tests. Yesterday we began our immunizations and also had a tuberculosis test.
>
> . . . I keep having doubts about my capability to serve, whether I want to or not, etc. Healthy, I suppose.
>
> The temperature ranges from a nighttime low of 80 to a daytime high of 88 and even higher humidity.

I drink about 2 gallons of liquid a day. Nights are
spent in underwear with no top sheet—which they
don't issue anyway, and I sweat all the time. We have
several Micronesians here and they say it is better
there.

    I am also somewhat ashamed of myself, as this is
the second week in a row I have missed church. I
will improve.

Just before I started training, Skip learned that he had
missed passing the draft-deferment exam by one point and
that the irregularity report the proctor had filed had not
been sent to his board, which reclassified him 1-A and thus
made him immediately draftable. After a hearing, he was
deferred to attend law school.

    His experience only highlighted what he called in a let-
ter to me "a frightening inequality in selection. A couple
of fellows there were drafted in spite of the appeal
because their pleas were not as verbose and/or dramatic
as others—I include myself in that deal. Thank your stars
you're in the Peace Corps because it's really getting hot
on the outside—1 2 guys at my camp [he was a counselor
all through high school and college] have notices—and
they're still in college!"

    A month after I reported to Key West, Skip entered
Albany Law School, in Albany, New York. When my training concluded at the end of October, I went to see my college girlfriend, whose home was near Albany, and so had a
chance to see Skip, as well. A week or two earlier in the
coal-mining village of Aberfan, Wales, thousands of tons of
waste from the Merthyr Vale Colliery piled atop the high

mountain by the village broke loose and slid into the valley. It was a school day and the children, after their morning assembly, at which they had sung "All Things Bright and Beautiful," were returning to their classrooms when the tsunami of black sludge overran twenty-one houses and the school before coming to rest. One hundred and sixteen children and five teachers were smothered— half the school.

The tragedy was still worldwide news. Although Skip and I had read about many disasters in our lives, this one struck a particular chord with both of us, and we were still shaken by it.

"How could a loving God allow this to happen?" he asked as we talked about the senseless and catastrophic loss. It was one of the seeming contradictions to our naïve, untested faith that neither of us had examined before and which neither of us could then answer.

A week later, my Peace Corps cohorts and I boarded a chartered plane in Oakland, California. After a stop for fuel in Honolulu, we landed on Guam at three a.m. in a torrential rain. We dashed across the tarmac and into a Quonset hut, where there were 150 uniformed soldiers our age about to go nonstop to Saigon. It was awkward and unpleasant. They looked silently at us, a bunch of informally dressed, freshly postcollege young men and women heading to what had been advertised as paradise. We looked silently at them. For me, anyway, there was guilt that they were heading to a war from which certainly many would not return, while we faced only the menace of hookworm.

At dawn, we boarded DC-4s—previously used in the

Berlin Airlift—to fly to our various districts, in my case six hundred miles south. When I stepped to the doorway after landing, there was a blast of warm, humid air and an overwhelming scent of decomposing vegetation from the palms, breadfruit trees, and vines that covered most of the island: nature in the raw. Virtually all the several thousand residents of Moen (now Weno), the main island and district center, were there to welcome us.

We landed on an airstrip made of crushed coral that had been bulldozed out of the shoreline. There was a mountain that rose perhaps twelve hundred feet, covered in palm and breadfruit trees. There were a few miles of dirt road (the island is only about ten square miles), on which Datsun pickup trucks hauled goods and people from place to place; a ride cost a dime. The administrative portion— which included an area called "American Hill," where Trust Territory officials lived—had electricity and running water, but most of the island had none. District and Trust Territory government buildings were one story and run down. There were Quonset huts left over from World War II, three of which I always visited when I was on Moen during the next two years. One housed the Truk Trading Company, run by a guy named Hank Chatroop, who picked up odd lots and bargains from around the world, duty-free. There were bicycle tires and cans of Dinty Moore beef stew; Japanese umbrellas and Johnnie Walker scotch; tins of German white asparagus and cans of mackerel that had been caught by Japanese fishermen just off the Truk Lagoon reef, sent to Japan for processing, then shipped back. Not as nutritious as fresh fish and many times more expensive, it nonetheless was a staple for those Trukese who could afford it. Another Quonset hut was a movie theater with a cement floor, wooden benches, and something only slightly better than a sheet for a screen; one of the most popular films was newsreel footage of the American bombing of the Japanese airfield on a small island in the lagoon. The Japanese had treated the Trukese brutally, and the islanders never tired of seeing their occupiers conquered. The third Quonset hut was the *imwoniwún piyé* (the house of drinking beer), where Trukese sat on stools, quaffing Sapporo or Budweiser at a long wooden bar, and interclan fights sometimes broke out. It had a cement floor, no decorations, and perfectly served its purpose. The American bureaucrats had a nicer place on the hill for dining and drinking, a sort of exiles officers' club with good-enough wooden furniture; volunteers could go, but often we drank with the locals.

For our few days of orientation before going to our assigned islands, I slept with three other volunteers on the dirt floor of an open-sided, thatch-roofed men's house, where our sleep was routinely interrupted by wandering pigs snuffling under our mosquito nets. The afternoon we arrived, I was told I had been assigned to one of the Western Islands, about as isolated a spot as there is on Earth, where on a clear day you can see another island. The small, flat Westerns had little exposure to the rest of the world and were then the most culturally traditional of the islands. Men wore only red cloth thongs; women, skirts handmade from hibiscus fiber or palm leaves. Once on the island, you left it only to fish in the large sailing canoes hollowed from breadfruit trees. My heart sank. I didn't mind going to Nowhere, but the prospect of being the only volunteer on a speck of land beyond Nowhere, a place where a supply ship came only every six weeks at best, seemed, well, to be honest, scary and very lonely. I was spared when my allergies to penicillin and sulfa drugs came to light, and for prudence I was assigned to be the only volunteer on Tsis Island in the lagoon, an hour by outboard-motor boat from Moen.

On the day we dispersed, I was gathered up by the chief and two other men from Tsis (pronounced *cease*) and, along with my trunk and the book locker given every Peace Corps volunteer, was loaded into an open twenty-two-foot boat with an eighteen-horsepower outboard engine and we set off. I would eventually become fluent in Trukese, but this day I still had only a beginner's grasp of it and communication was labored and involved many gestures. I understood more than I could speak, so my conversation was limited pretty much to basic necessities. As we plied our way across the lagoon, the men touched my clothes, closely examined my tanned skin—lighter than theirs—and rummaged through my trunk and book locker with unselfconscious curiosity. I tried to stifle the sudden notion that all this "right hand washing the left" stuff we had learned in training was idealistic fantasy and that the main course for the supposed welcoming party on the island was going to be me in a pot.

After about forty-five minutes, we pulled up at a long dock on an island called Fefan. (The Trukese word *fefan* means "woman," and the narrow, three-mile-long island with two peaks a few hundred feet high resembles a woman—a very big woman—lying on her back.) A white man in a white robe, followed by a German shepherd, came running along the dock; we had stopped so I could be shown off to the Jesuit missionary for the area. The Jesuits had been in Micronesia for decades and many Trukese were Catholics, especially on the five islands in this part of the lagoon. They also ran Xavier High School on Moen, where they taught students from all over Truk. (Protestant missionaries also had large congregations in other areas of Truk, and Micronesia.) He grasped my hand and spoke rapidly in what I knew to be English but which was peppered with Trukese and grammatically constructed like Latin, so there was a lot of information to absorb before he got to the verbs at the end of the sentences. His name was Andrew Connolly, a graduate of Fordham University, in New York. His dog's name was Nakkich, the Trukese word for rat.

I was the first outsider to live on Tsis. The Trukese word denotes the sound of a woman walking in a grass skirt; it also is the name of the overhang at the entrance to an *ut,* a men's house, and our small island was geographically situated like an overhang for Fefan, at its southern end. These islands were about twelve miles from the outer reef of the lagoon. Though small, Tsis was prominent in legend. The residents of Tsis, Fefan, and another small island nearby were known as the Mácheweyichchún. Great warriors, brothers, lived on Tsis and had claim to all the surrounding reef islands and the largest island in the lagoon, twenty-five miles away.

The first association I made when I saw Tsis was of a Victorian shoe. One end was a hill perhaps a hundred feet high; the other was a foot above sea level. It was no more than a quarter of a square mile in size and, I quickly learned, could be walked around in forty minutes. There was no electricity and there were no roads or bikes. The paths were a few feet wide at most. One went around the island; others cut across its narrow girth. The western end of the island, where the school was, had a beautiful white sand beach, the second-nicest in the lagoon. Rainwater for drinking and general use was captured in a variety of buckets and barrels, including old fifty-five-gallon oil drums. A tiny spring at the high end of the island flowed into two little pools: a small top one for drinking, a slightly larger one beneath it for bathing and for washing clothes. Huts were almost always made of local materials and had dirt floors; one or two had cement floors and corrugated-tin sides and roofs. When I disembarked on the grassy communal earth and rock dock, I noticed how much detritus there was—palm leaves, coconut husks, and sea- and wind-borne stuff littered the water that lapped the rocky shore—and once again was struck by the overpowering scent of decomposing flora, though I stopped noticing it within a day and it never registered again. On one side at the end of the dock was the men's house, a fifteen-by-thirty-foot open structure with breadfruit tree timbers for posts and beams and a woven-leaf peaked roof to shield the dirt floor from rain. On the other side of the dock was a small rectangular hut constructed from what looked to be a dozen different things: my home.

As for the welcoming party, I was, in fact, the dinner

guest and not the dinner. The meal was laid out in the men's house. All 185 residents of the island were there. The women and children stood outside the house, while the men sat in a circle, squatting like baseball catchers or, in my case, because my knees couldn't stand it for long, seated with legs crossed. In front of each of us was a freshly cut banana leaf, on which were helpings of taro, preserved breadfruit, a whole roasted fish, a bit of boiled chicken, and a mound of rice, all of which we ate with our right hands. This was a lean season for food and so this meal was a feast. Ceremonial meals in Truk require ceremonial speeches, which are at once apologetic (for what has been provided, no matter how splendid), flowery (compliments are mandatory), and long (not much else to do). They went on for an hour and a half and then it was my turn. I stumbled along, saying how grateful I was for the hospitality, giving thanks for the delicious meal, and making clear that I was there to work for everyone on the island. This latter part was important, because the island's thirty-five families were divided into seven clans, each jealous of the others for one thing or another. The greatest mistake I could have made would have been to appear to favor one clan over another. For this reason, my hut was on communal land.

"My house (rent free) is right on the water," I wrote my parents.

Sand floor, half of it covered with raised board, about two inches high. That is the sleeping area. The size of the whole thing is (maybe) 20' x 10'. It is

constructed of corrugated tin, woven rupung leaves
(like palms but twice as wide), chicken wire, old
screen, and a couple of breadfruit wood timbers.
I have to do a little more construction on it but as a
whole it is quite nice by Trukese standards. The view
from my screenless 2-foot by 2-foot window—there
is a corrugated-tin flap I can pull down when it
rains—is of the island of Fefan, about ¾ mile away.

Tsis is a small island and is plagued by bad water
and little food because it is both lower than the
other islands (and therefore hasn't a mountain that
can provide a good stream) and small, making food
a problem this time of year. But it is a beautiful
place—very lush and typical tropical islandish. The
school is a 10-minute walk to the east—no, west—
and is built beside a lovely white sandy beach. I am
teaching 5th and 6th grade English as a Second
Language and math, plus adult education. There
are 15 kids combined; 6th grade is the end of
classes. The school, newly constructed by the Truk
administration and made of cinder block, is the
only cement-based building on the island and is
the sturdiest. There is a half-finished cinder-block
cookhouse. Work stopped on it when the school
was finished; don't ask me why, as no answer I've
had makes sense. We will finish building it whenever
I can get the materials, so the children can get
administration rice and have a lunch. There are only
5 people on the island who understand any English
at all. So far I seem to be getting on well. Last night I

was asked if I would stay after my 21 months were
up. I told them I had only been here two days and
that after a year they might want me to go.

The first week I was on Tsis, Andy Connolly came over
in his outboard-powered boat for a meal. He was delighted
to learn that my father was a priest and asked all about
him. He hoped I would come over for services whenever
I wanted, though of course, he quickly added, because I
wasn't a Catholic, I wouldn't be allowed to receive Communion. (When Henry VIII seceded from Rome and
formed the Church of England —virtually Catholic but
with no fealty to the Pope— Anglicans became unworthy
of Christ's Supper.) Ah, well. I'd figured that might be the
case, but I found myself disappointed anyway. It was hard
to imagine God was so particular that exceptions couldn't
be made about something so important, when the closest
place for me to have Communion was six hundred miles
across open ocean. To me, the rite was a symbolic communion between God and me, or whoever partook, and it
was so much a part of my life and an article of my faith that
being denied it was being denied something comforting,
precious, and beneficial to my spiritual health. (Though I
was disqualified from receiving Communion in the
Catholic Church, it welcomed me to acknowledge my
sins. "Late yesterday it suddenly struck me that Ash
Wednesday was to follow in a few hours," I wrote to my
parents in February. "Fr. Connolly came over for an hour
yesterday for the imposition of ashes, and since there
seemed to be nothing to prohibit my partaking, I did. It's

too bad there are no facilities for getting to church here, as it would do me some good to go—having not made my Communion since early November.")

Theology aside, I quickly became friends with Andy. He was about forty, with a ruddy complexion and graying hair. He kept himself trim with a daily jog, what he called "the only culturally acceptable dance for the padre." Sometimes he would pick me up in his boat to go to Moen, where he got around on an old Vespa motor scooter, his white robe fluttering in the breeze, a big smile on his face, no helmet on his head. I went over to Fefan to visit him every few weeks. We'd have dinner and a few glasses of scotch and talk long into the night. He lived in a two-story tropical-style house beside a huge mango tree that was next to the mission church built by Spanish Jesuits. When he came in the mid-1950s, he joined a Spanish priest named Jaime, who had been there for decades. When Jaime died a few years before my arrival, he was buried under the mango tree, a favorite of his. On my first visit to Andy's, I couldn't help but notice a set of false teeth he used as a paperweight. He saw the puzzled look on my face.

"They were Jaime's," he said nonchalantly. "They make a good keepsake."

Within only a month or two, this no longer seemed strange, which is perhaps an indication of how by necessity we acclimate ourselves to unaccustomed circumstances.

Five

After a lifetime of America's version of civilization, Tsis took a lot of getting used to. I slept on a mat of woven leaves. The toilet was a leaf-sided shed fifteen feet from shore, which I walked to on what at first seemed like a tightrope in the form of a fallen coconut tree. There were two holes in the floor and what went through them was flushed twice a day by the tides. Often I would find a kid with a handline inside, angling for one of the fish that were attracted. At first, I limited myself to one meal a day because with the seasonal food shortage, that was all anyone else on the island was able to have. ("No one ever starves," I wrote to my parents, "but very few have much excess weight.") I also had a stash of canned goods that, with part of my ninety-dollar-a-month living allowance, I had picked up at the Truk Trading Company to supplement what I bought from people on the island or was given to me. I made do communicating in Trukese and found necessity was an inducement to expanding my vocabulary quickly. My English-teaching duties took only half a day, which left time for taking a census of the island, which all volunteers were doing for the Trust Territory government. It was a tremendously useful way for me to put together the complicated clan relationships of the islanders, as well as have a list of everyone's names so I could learn them. I also made plans with the chief and the island council for projects. A few days after I arrived, I suggested that, with the water shortage, perhaps we could dig a well, which everyone quickly agreed to, though for a number of reasons it soon turned into an impractical exercise and all we had to show for our work was a hole with constantly collapsing sides and a flotilla of rats that had fallen in and drowned. Only later did I discover that the reason everyone showed enthusiasm was because they thought it was what I wanted to do and they wanted to be polite; they had tried and failed before with a well. It took a while before I was able to look at projects through their eyes rather than my own. What finally taught me to put aside my standards of utility and aesthetics was an explanation for my benefit by the chief during a meeting of the island council a month after I arrived. The council was eager for me to try to help them find funding to replace the woven-rupung-leaf roof of the men's house with corrugated tin.

"But what you have has worked for countless generations," I argued, pointing up at the sticks, an inch in diameter, that had long leaves folded over them, held on by palm-leaf spines stitched through them. "It's traditional. And it looks a lot better than a roof made from tin."

"That's what it seems to you," the chief said patiently. "But we have to replace the leaves every year or two and it takes a lot of work. Tin lasts for years. For us, it's progress."

I stopped romanticizing the island, as if it were a *National Geographic* photo spread, and began to see it as the work in progress it was.

My sense of isolation from all I knew was ever present. As we were just seven degrees north of the equator, day and night were almost of equal length. The sun set in Technicolor splendor. The stars that followed in a sky that stretched to 180 degrees of horizon formed a celestial carpet of uncountable twinkling white dots that seemed to hang so low, I felt that if I stood up in a hurry, I would bang my head against the universe. My battery-powered short-wave radio picked up the British Broadcasting Service in Papua, New Guinea, a thousand miles to the south, but there was no radio on the island for us to call for help from Moen, eight miles away, in an emergency. Rain fell not only in sheets but in entire bedding ensembles. After a storm, mosquitoes bred in water-filled coconut shells and brackish puddles; when the wind blew, they were not much of a problem, but on still nights, I had several foul-smelling Japanese-manufactured green coils of repellent burning on the sand floor to help fend them off. The constant high humidity fostered a recurring fungal outbreak in a particularly sensitive spot. Every letter to my parents in my first weeks contained a plea for more medical samples of Tinactin, the one thing that brought at least some relief. I found myself withdrawing, the result of what we had been forewarned in training would be likely attacks of culture shock. When I counted how many more months remained in my tour, and there were periods when I did it every day, it seemed I'd be there forever, and my spirits sank even lower. I spoke Trukese aloud all day but carried on incessant conversations in English in my head. I noted in my diary that I had become a stellar interior monologuist but a lousy conversationalist. Andy Connolly's English now sounded perfectly correct.

There were, however, short periods when I was at least partially back in the life I had always known. The first came on Thanksgiving Day, two weeks after my arrival on Tsis. The day before, a message arrived from the two volunteers and the three contract teachers on the neighboring island of Uman, three miles of choppy water away, that I should get myself over for a real Thanksgiving meal. Uman was half the size of Fefan, which was ten times or more the size of Tsis. Both islands had contract teachers, hired by the Trust Territory government, who had been given what by local standards was luxury housing in cinder-block homes that had generators, stoves, and "showers so big, they could be used for curling rinks if they were frozen over," I wrote to my parents. Peace Corps volunteers did the same work in the school but lived under local conditions. Going from my hut to the splendor of a contract teacher's home, in which he produced a turkey, stuffing, and all-trimmings meal, was like being in a space warp. No longer was I in Micronesia, but, rather, in an alternative American reality. The moment I walked out of the house, however, my return trip was complete.

On Christmas Eve, I went with many people from Tsis to Fefan for church. Virtually everyone on Tsis was Catholic, but because there were only two outboard-powered boats on the island, attendance at services on Fefan was limited to particularly holy days. Andy Connolly came over every month or so to conduct a well-attended service in the small church on Tsis, but otherwise Sundays passed without formal worship and the church went unused between his pastoral visits. While the Trukese were devout, they were devout in their own way, which is to say that they didn't put all their ecclesiastical fish in one creel. It was common for a Catholic who wanted a divorce to turn Protestant suddenly, or for marriage to induce a switch from one denomination to the other. Though religion was taken seriously, the theological intricacies of both Catholicism and Protestantism and the differences between them were hardly understood by most Trukese. (A common reply on a Sunday to "Where are you going?" was "To fool the padre.") And while the traditional island beliefs in spirits, magic, and sorcery were no longer predominant, they still had a place in daily life. For instance, a devout Catholic would be concerned about a pregnant woman walking at night in a certain part of Uman, because that was where the chicken ghost lived, which could harm the fetus. And while the Trukese were happy to be vaccinated and take Western medicines, when someone was really ill, they would stay at home and be treated by traditional methods. The hospital was considered a place you went to die, which, to a point, was true.

I was glad to be at the Christmas Eve service, even if I

couldn't really be part of it. It was odd, however—as if I had been welcomed into a home at dinnertime but not invited to the table. Still, I liked being back in church. There was enough similarity in the Catholic service to remind me of all the Christmas Eve services I had been part of at home, though there was more choreography than I was used to, and the part where many people kissed a doll meant to be the baby Jesus was a bit much. I slept comfortably at the mission in an extra room with an army-surplus metal bed frame and mattress, and the next day I accompanied Andy as he took Communion to an old woman who was dying. We tramped the trail behind a Trukese acolyte ringing a bell.

One of my happiest memories of Tsis is the day several months after I arrived that I checked in with a family whose baby had a serious and worsening respiratory infection. For days, I had been unable to convince them to take him to the hospital on Moen, because they had more confidence in traditional medicine, which included various bits of flora being thrown into a pot on the fire and a blanket put over the baby's head to allow him to inhale the steamy fumes. The baby looked near death and the family was softly wailing in fear of it. I had hoped the island medicine would work, but it was clear that it hadn't. I cajoled and then begged the parents to let me take the baby to Moen, and to my relief, they agreed. I asked a good friend, who owned one of the two boats, for a ride. It was a stormy day with high seas, but even so, most of the family insisted on going along, which meant there were at least ten of us in the open twenty-two-foot boat. It was so packed and thus rode so low that water kept pouring over the gunnels, so we bailed constantly. Then, having left traditional cures behind, the family insisted we cover all bets and stop at the mission so Andy could bless the baby, who was looking worse by the minute. The trip to Moen took over three hours. Doctors immediately began treatment, and a week later we took the baby home. The doctors said if we had arrived an hour or two later, he would have been dead of pneumonia.

There was a growing social challenge on Tsis that was not without comedy. Adolescent sex was both permissible and expected; by the time both boys and girls were sixteen, most had considerable sexual experience. Other than incest taboos, there were few restrictions, apart from not allowing multiple affairs to become a scandal. Marriages played out in the open, but there were "friendships" that played in secret. It didn't matter that the island was so small that it was impossible to do anything in secret, but so long as activity was not seen, it was deemed unknown. This behavior was so common that not long after my arrival, people began to tell me that they were concerned that I had no "friend."

"You're not like the padre on Fefan, who has vowed to be single," one said.

"You'll offend the women of the island if you don't pick one," said another. "They'll be mad at you."

Trukese women generally wore fairly shapeless hand-stitched cotton dresses or muumuus, though many of the girls and occasionally some of the women wore skirts of hibiscus fiber or palm leaves, or a wraparound piece of cotton fabric, and nothing else. There were two kinds of feminine beauty. A young woman who had reached puberty and just beyond was called a *ttipwúk* (pronounced *teapook*). *Ttipwúk*s were generally slender, and because they often wore only skirts, their physical changes were easy to see and were readily admired by the men on the island. But as a woman grew older, her physiognomy grew a bit thicker. Beauty after the late teens was registered on a different scale. If a woman was heavier, it meant that she came from a family with enough coconut and breadfruit trees (every tree had an owner) to supply, buy (from the sale of copra), or trade for enough food to eat well. Thick thighs were prized. The great compliment when speaking of a woman's beauty was to say that she had *pecheen weewee chék angaarap*—"legs like a tuna fish."

In the gloaming before a full-moon night perhaps three months after I arrived, the wind was down, the lagoon was calm, and the single men were lying about the men's house, singing Trukese love songs, which have a plaintive quality not unlike American country music: "No true love without pain," one goes, "and no true pain without love." Another begins, "Open, open the door to your heart, and I will come in." I was about to cook a piece of fresh parrot fish someone had given me, when I heard a commotion outside my hut. I opened the door, to find easily one hundred people, including what I realized were all the single young women on the island. One of my friends spoke for the group. "We worry about you," he said. "You need company. You need to pick someone."

I didn't say anything for a minute as the absurdity and

the potential danger of the moment sunk in. Who gets a knock on his door to find he is being offered his choice of available women? But I immediately knew the hazard that came with a choice, because I would no longer be seen as the volunteer for the island, but, rather, as the volunteer for the clan of the woman I chose, and I would not be as trusted. I said thank you but no as graciously as I could. After everyone left, I went back into my hut, at once laughing and shaking. Although I had had a steady succession of girlfriends from sixteen on, what had helped me with my choice, and what I did not tell anyone on Tsis, was that adolescent sex was neither permissible nor expected in my house, and my parents' steely prohibition against premarital relations—my father's sharpest warning to me was that I had better not make anyone pregnant—had rubbed off on me. I intended to refrain until I married. (However, the sexual revolution of the 1960s, which did not really begin until after I joined the Peace Corps, eventually enlisted me.)

For my first several months on Tsis, this incident and so much else meant that I was an oddity to the people, who nonetheless treated me kindly and generously, someone always coming by with a piece of fresh fish or cooked breadfruit. Almost daily, an adult or child would present me with a *mwárámwár,* a garland of flowers that fit like a band around my head. I was an object of incessant curiosity to the children, one or more of whom were always peering through the holes in the siding of my hut to see what I was doing. When I awoke in the morning, they often were there, as they were when I cooked or read or napped. They called out to me from trees like parrots as I walked the trail to school: "Hello!" "How are you?" My loss of privacy unnerved me, but I was nothing special in this regard: Small islands led to a culture where there *was* no privacy.

The difficult adjustment to Trukese life and my sense of loneliness and isolation from all I knew reached a crescendo in February, about four months after I arrived. It had been windless for days and the mosquitoes were even more ubiquitous than the kids. Even three smoking coils were not enough to keep the insects from bombarding me in my hut. They were so bad that at 8:00 p.m. I crawled under the mosquito netting that dropped over my sleeping mat. A while later, the wind grew very strong, a sign that a big storm was about to hit. When it did, water pelted my hut with such force that a small leak opened above my feet. I moved them to a dry spot, but another opened over my legs. I found another position that was dry, until a hole opened over my head and I was drenched as if by a hose.

"That's it!" I yelled to no one. "I don't have to put up with this! Mrs. Lax's little boy wasn't raised only to drown in bed. I quit!"

And then I broke out in near-hysterical laughter as it struck me that there was no one to quit *to*. There was no radio for calling in my resignation, and even if there had been, there was no way off the island in this storm.

I had a wet, fitful sleep and awoke at dawn to quiet. The storm had passed, the wind had ceased, but inside, I was in tumult. I knew I had to get off the island. A married couple had arrived a week earlier in the second group of volunteers to come, and I decided I needed to meet them—immediately. I put on my daily wardrobe of khaki shorts and a faded blue work shirt and was heading toward the water to swim the three-quarters of a mile across deep, choppy, fast-current sea to where they were when a voice asked in Trukese where I was going. It was an islander several years older than I, with whom I had forged a friendship.

"Fefan," I said.

"You're going to swim?" he asked, at once amused and concerned.

"Yes," I said, suddenly aware of the silliness of my intent.

"There's a canoe right here that you could take," he reminded me, pointing to one made from a hollowed bread fruit tree trunk with an outrigger that was at my disposal.

"Oh, right."

"Or I can just take you in my boat." He had one of the two outboard motorboats on the island. (It was he who took the sick baby to Moen.)

"Thank you. I'd appreciate that," I said as my panic lessened.

Twenty minutes later, I found my way to the door of the hut that people at the mission had made for the volunteers. It was 7:00 a.m. Both the husband and wife answered my knock. I introduced myself.

"You look like you could use a drink," he said.

"I expect I could," I replied, never before having had a drink in the morning.

The Johnnie Walker and the conversation that accompanied it started to calm me down over the next hour, but it was two days before I was ready to go back to my solitary life on Tsis.

In time, I adapted. I wrote voluminous letters to friends, who kindly kept writing back, although at first I found that a number of them praised me for what I was doing for these supposedly benighted people, as if I were bringing them the benefits of American civilization.

"You have it backward," I would tell them. "There's one of me with something to share, and there are 185 people on Tsis with something to give me. I'm the one who's benefiting the most."

My parents sent me a battery-powered tape recorder at my request, along with recordings of various pieces of classical and other music I asked for. I also used the recorder for voice letters to Skip and to them. I added community-development work to my teaching and, now better attuned to what the people on Tsis really wanted and needed, scrounged up government money to buy cement so we could build a seawall to keep the ocean from the island's taro patch, and for other projects, as well.

After six months on Tsis, I felt like a local. When the calendar showed only eleven months remained, it suddenly seemed I'd be leaving in weeks. But by then I had another concern. I feared, along with other volunteers I talked with, that all we were doing to try to help might in the end make life worse for the Trukese. What would happen once the inevitable neon signs and tourists made it to Moen and then the islands in the lagoon? Peace Corps volunteers

Conferring with islanders, 1967

were advertised as "agents of change." I worried we could be more like double agents who did more harm than good, and that by coming to paradise, we'd turn it into paradise lost.

During all the time I was in Truk, my coming battle with my draft board over whether I would be accepted as a conscientious objector was a steady presence. I read the prayer book and Bible to find quotes to support my argument in the statement I would have to write for my draft board. I read Gandhi and bought pacifist texts, including a manual from the American Friends Service Committee that spelled out in specific detail both arguments for pacifism and the consequences of prison. Federal prisoners, I learned, receive at Christmas a brown paper bag holding cigarettes and hard candy. Many nights a week, my nightmare of being in prison played itself out, with small variations, all disquieting.

And all through this time, my parents and I conversed

by letter about matters of church and state. "I do not know whether or not to get into prolonged ideological disputes over the morality or properness of the war in Vietnam, or anywhere for that matter," I replied after they had written that they saw no course but to follow the president.

> In this instance, I think we have been wrong from the beginning and should have realized it 13 years ago. I cannot see why we regard ourselves as International Policemen of Justice and Democracy when, among other things, we are doing such a poor job at home. I can hardly find anything in the Sermon on the Mount, which I have always understood to be a pretty representative example, or even classic example, of Christian thought, that suggests there is something "right" about marching off to war. I do not see, when we follow the teachings of a man who put the ear back on a servant of the high priest (and what is any soldier, ours or theirs, hmmm?) after it was cut off, how we can drop napalm on other servants . . . and certainly the parallel of ideologies cannot be that far-fetched. Yet I do not profess to have an answer at all. Still, I can only do what I believe right when that belief is based on something other than the law of man. I do believe there is a solution other than prolonged battle to a standstill, and I believe Mr. Johnson has not been honest to the goals he set forth only a year ago. I am convinced he is coming to the point, or has already reached it, where nothing

short of total victory will suffice. In short, I do not
agree when you say, "We cannot do otherwise." I
think we can and I know we should.

. . . Kindly remember that when I speak I
speak only for myself and for what I believe to be
right for me. I am incapable of doing otherwise or
expecting others to do so at present. I agree; wars
are never justified. But people keep saying this
while holding a dove in one hand and a sword in
the other. Most every war I have read about has
been due in large measure to gross miscalculations
and communications breakdowns between the
protagonists. If we put down our swords long
enough to communicate, if we put them down long
enough to understand, then there would never be
an instance of passing by the other side while our
neighbor is attacked and killed. Unfortunately we
are attacked by the two mortalities: earthly and
heavenly. I cannot reconcile the two. I realize Hitler
was a maniac, and I realize the rest of the world
was turned into maniacs fighting him. I cannot
believe that is the answer, to stop the bully with
his own force. It is either right to kill a man or it
isn't. Human life, life in general, is absolute. It
either exists or it doesn't. We either make it or we
don't. We either have a right, and sometimes even
an obligation, to take it away or we don't. It does
exist, not by our making, and is not subject to
our discrimination as to who shall and who shall
not. "Judge not lest ye be judged . . ." "Let him

who is without sin cast the first stone . . ." etc. &
etc. & etc.

We seem bent on saving the Vietnamese even if
we have to destroy them and their country to do it.
I still cannot reconcile the two theories: War is
wrong, but then we have to meet force with force.
And force begets force and on into eternity. My
"cause" [as my mother put it, not unkindly] is
most likely an impossible one, yet if I follow my
conscience it is all I can do. And someday enough
other people will see that war is futile and defeating,
and that "victories" are really negative entities, that
destruction is not the way to understanding how to
bring an end to war. The war to end all wars has
been fought too many times to make me believe a
path of war will ever bring peace. I hope you will
continue writing and sending cookies if I go to
prison, an unsavory topic which shall be dealt with
at a later date.

If I do join the priesthood, it will not be for a
number of years (as if my say had much to do
with it). I imagine I will continue in some sort
of "service" capacity.

What, pray tell, is the New Morality anyway?

It was a year before I was able to attend an Episcopal
service and take Communion, an eternity for someone
who had seldom missed more than one Sunday in the past.
For my three weeks of vacation, I left my small island to go
to other, larger small islands in Micronesia, and made sure
that I ended up on Guam on Christmas Eve so that I could

go to St. John's Church. ("I find it a bit ironic," I wrote my parents, "going to church on Christmas, praying for peace on Earth, goodwill, etc.; when the church is on Guam, where so many bombers are stationed and where so many troops pass thru. But then, I suppose there isn't a better place, is there, for reminding people of that? So much for moralizing.") I don't recall ever wanting more to be part of a service than I had that one, nor feeling better after one, and in retrospect, it may be that my feelings that night were the apogee of my faith.

In many of my letters to my parents, I wrote about what I saw going on in the Church. The ecumenical movement was on the rise then, and my relegation to the spectator section at Andy's services drove home a feeling that more was made of theological differences than was necessary. In one letter I asked what all the commotion was about— I cleverly began it, "For Christ's sake!"; to me, Christians had basically the same faith but practiced it by different means. My father replied in a two-page typed letter that he found my thoughts "most interesting" and went on to explain why he felt I was misguided.

> While I agree with you in general, I must disagree with your statement that we basically have the same faith, and differ only in the means.
>
> First, let us agree that truth is not centered in the Anglican Church, nor in the Roman Church, nor in any other church, but let us also agree that certain facets of each church have been pushed to the foreground and out of context.
>
> To illustrate this, we know, if we have any

intelligence at all, that salvation does not lie through the See of St. Peter, nor through the Apostolic Succession, nor through the Sacraments, nor through any one thing. Salvation (and I don't mean going to heaven, but rather that we might live as the sons of God, which we are, rather than the sons of Satan, which we are not) is only to be gained when we learn that true faith is to accept the statements of Our Lord concerning God, in their fullness. We cannot, as we have done, take a part and build a religion on it. The R.C.s have taken the text "Thou art Peter . . ." and pushed it into a religion in itself which excludes all others, and claim that salvation can only come through the Apostolic Succession, and the Anglican Church, excepting the Pope, holds the same to be true. The Baptists have taken the view that every man is his own savior, and when he is converted, this is something he does for God, rather than vice versa. They also take as their God the God of the Old Testament, and at least the Southern Baptists have taken the incident in Genesis where Agar and Ishmael are cast out, in order to foster the teaching that, as Agar and Ishmael are the ancestors of all Negroes, to give the Negro equality is to flout the very word and will of God.

This is what we have done. But Our Lord said simply that "God is Love," and proved it many times. When we realise the greatness of this, we find it all-encompassing . . . even to the honest Atheist and the dishonest Christian. Christ showed us that the

love of God is so great that there is no sin which He
condemns except the sin of hypocrisy. How often
do you read "Thy sins be forgiven thee"? Even to
the woman taken in adultery He said "Neither do
I condemn thee . . . go in peace and sin no more."
[Luke 7:50] But to the Pharisees and scribes, "Woe
unto you Scribes, Pharisees, Hypocrites. For you
shut up the kingdom of heaven against men; for you
neither go in yourselves, nor do you allow those
who are entering to go in. . . . Ye make clean the
outside of the cup, but inside it is full of iniquity
and dead men's bones." [Matthew 23:25, loosely
quoted.]

Here, then, to me at least, is the beginning. First,
we must cease to be hypocrites, and then we must
learn the equally hard lesson that there is a goodness
in those with whom we do not agree. In short, I
must learn to have a concern for those outside the
faith, even the R.C.s, who, by excluding all outside
their faith, don't realize that, by this very action,
they have excluded Our Lord, no matter how
much they may lay claim to Him. Nor the Southern
Baptists who, by turning a text of Scripture to their
own use, have negated all that He lived and died for.
Nor the Anglicans, who smugly imply "I am white,
I am Anglican, I was born in Holy Wedlock, I am
Republican, and therefore I have everything."

When and if we get to heaven, the honest Atheist
will find that God will probably say "You were
mistaken, but come in." But to the lip-service

Christian, and the people who attend Mass and
Holy Communion each Holy Day, and hate the
Negroes and others, I can imagine the eyes of God
flashing and a repetition of Our Lord's words to
the Pharisees.

What we need, Son, apart from a good typist, is
first to sit down and study what God is like, not
what I can give or you can give, until we find a God
who pleases us, but having found that God is Love,
then try and bring that love into the soul of
mankind.

How am I going to love the Jehovah's Witnesses,
who say that the greatest joy in heaven will be to
watch the sufferings of the damned in hell? Or the
others, including ourselves?

Should we try any Ecumenical Movement apart
from this foundation that God is Love, we shall be
like the whale, who upset a boat and swallowed a
R.C. missionary, an Anglican Priest, a Methodist
Minister and a Baptist Preacher, and then went and
had a good Ecumenical movement.

Not the means, Son, but the basic knowledge of
God is where we differ.

Skip was also a steady correspondent, and wrote my
parents, too. His letters to me were funny, acerbic, full of
news of mutual friends, and at once loving and flip. They
were a great emotional lift; it was as if we were back in our
dorm room, wisecracking with each other. One began,
"Dear Daddy's Little Wonder"; another ended, "Stay love-

able"; a third was signed, "Love and kisses, Erle Stanley Gardner." I also signed mine with various aliases, among them Alexander Selkirk, the eighteenth-century Scottish castaway who supposedly was the inspiration for *Robinson Crusoe.*

In June 1967, a seven-page letter from Skip, handwritten on notebook paper, arrived. He covered a dozen things, from girlfriends to law school to college friends, but in the middle of it, he was clearly aware that the only thing between the army and him was passing his courses:

> My exams went pretty well but sadly or realistically
> no one is sure whether they'll be back next year.
> Was a pretty bad scene after our last exam, everyone
> saying goodbye for the last time. Looking at it now it
> seems particularly funny because I couldn't recall
> any great fraternal bonds forming between any of
> us—rather a stainless steel–like schedule: 1. Get up.
> 2. Eat. 3. Study. 4. Eat. 5. Study. And so on. Albany
> is no womblike atmosphere [like Hobart] but at
> least you're *inside,* but too, almost outside. Inside,
> expanding your mind to the point and past the
> point of bursting, but outside eyeing with no great
> anticipation the possibility of raising an M-16,
> pointing it at a living, breathing, human being
> and snuffing out his life with no interaction,
> introduction—nothing. . . .

He spent the summer at the Boy Scouts camp on Long Island where he had worked for many summers, but by then his life had changed drastically. Just about the time I finally settled into Truk, he quickly had to acclimatize to unaccustomed circumstances of his own. His exams did not go as well as he'd thought, and he flunked out of Albany Law School. Knowing he now would be drafted, he considered his alternatives and chose to enlist in the army and go to Officer Candidate School. While I soldiered on as a Peace Corps volunteer, he soldiered on as a soldier. And as I dived deeper and deeper into my feelings as a conscientious objector and thought about the statement I would eventually have to give my draft board on why my religious training and belief led me to my position, he found his own faith put to a test, and was deeply changed.

It was four months before I heard from Skip again. When he wrote, he said he had joined the army instead of another service because he liked the outdoors and the camaraderie he had experienced as a Boy Scout. He liked passing on the expert ability he had developed to track animals in the wild, and this seemed another version of that. What he did not add is that he became a specialist in a field that allowed no room for error. He was sent to OCS at Fort Benning, Georgia, where instructors slyly measured leadership ability through various challenges. Instructors generally rode their students hard, but Skip breezed through, hardly giving his tasks a second thought, and found himself wondering why his superiors did not challenge him more. Later he learned it was because he scored very high on the leadership scale, leadership in that environment being to get people to have confidence in you so that you can bind them into a problem-solving unit able to choose the most functional means forward.

He attended church regularly while at Fort Benning, he later said, "to find a place of security. OCS is an awful experience. It's not quite as awful as basic training, which I did at Fort Dix, but in its way it's awful. And what do you know, lo and behold, there is an Episcopal service at 7:00 a.m. I dragged myself to it sleepy-eyed and was covered in the blanket of coziness that the liturgy gives you. I felt the same kind of knot in my stomach from hunger."

"Like everyone at OCS," he wanted to be assigned to military intelligence or personnel, "but that's not where they needed the bodies. You could go into the combat arms or armor. I picked infantry because I liked walking. They told me that I could transfer to something else, but that was silly."

It was especially silly after his superiors saw where he excelled. In the week of OCS devoted to setting ambushes and patrolling, he proved so capable that, unlike most of his classmates, he was not sent to Vietnam after he graduated. Rather, the army kept him at Fort Benning, as an instructor in ambush and patrol, where in the next year he trained over one thousand men. Forty years later, he still was slightly bemused by where the army had placed him, though not by his capabilities: "They assigned me, of all people, to become an instructor of ambushing. I taught it for a year prior to going to Vietnam. I did it every day in every kind of weather you can think of, in every kind of swamp you can think of, in Alabama. I've seen more snakes and eaten more snakes . . . I just knew how to do silence in the jungles and to move against a profile."

He did not, however, tell me this at the time. He did write to say that after OCS he had married his senior-year sweetheart, one of my closest college friends. Her father was an Episcopal priest and she hoped Skip would become one, a notion that he carried but was undecided about. As for his duties at Fort Benning, he reported simply that he was being kept on as an instructor. Perhaps I was distracted by the good news of the marriage, but for whatever reason, I didn't think to ask, "An instructor of *what?*" and he didn't tell me. His ensuing letters were vague regarding the details of his army life. One, written on University of Indiana stationery, began: "Well, here I am, studying bladder control at the university."

Decades later, he detailed his army work. "At ambush sites what matters is to blend into the environment and do nothing to attract attention. You use tape to secure your battle rattle, the sound of the various metal paraphernalia— canteens, grenades, shovel and so on. The army has gone to plastics now but then we carried a lot of metal that could brush against each other and make an unnatural noise, and you don't want to make an unnatural noise that gives a straight line to anyone. What I learned was a hybrid of Boy Scouts tracking, what I picked up on the street, and basic Ranger stuff—breathing techniques and other means of keeping absolute silence in the jungle, because the first person who breaks the silence has given up his life."

While he learned the techniques of the Rangers, the army's elite fighting force, he contrived to avoid going to Ranger School and, in fact, trained Rangers. "The Ranger

training command had two parts," he explains. "Snuffies
and deadbeats who everybody knew were headed for Vietnam. [A Snuffy is a knucklehead, named after the World
War II comic strip character Snuffy Smith, a moonshining
hillbilly who joins the army after growing weary of being
chased by revenue agents.] These were guys who lifted
weights during breaks, had no necks. There was the expectation that I would be a Ranger and train like a Ranger, but
I was always kind of postponing and avoiding having them
send me to Ranger School. So every day I trained people
how to ambush. It was a little like an idiot savant doing one
thing well, and I don't mean to take a shot at idiot savants
I didn't go to Ranger School, but everybody referred to
me as a Ranger." He shrugged. "Call me Elmer Fudd if you
want to."

For the many summers that Skip worked at Camp
Wauwepex, the Boy Scouts camp, he learned and taught
animal tracking and finding one's way in the wilderness. In
many of the ways he managed his younger Scouts, he handled his recruits as they had their first encounter with the
wild. Army reservists or college Reserve Office Training
Corps students would arrive in the predawn, with little
clue of what awaited. Then they were driven far into the
remote rough countryside of Alabama and unloaded.

"I would have a platoon of these rumdums who didn't
know anything," he recalled. "The army had rented these
huge tracts of land that went over mountains and valleys
and swamps, all kinds of stuff. I liked it because it was out
in nature. I thought I'd died and gone to heaven. We'd have
them out there for ten days maybe, sometimes longer."

It was not a case of whipping his trainees into shape:

" 'Whipping into shape' is something you say around the fire. It was just getting them from one place to another on the grid. The job was to keep them on the azimuth [compass bearing]. When you're doing this at night and it's raining, it's a pain. And I have to tell you, it snows in Alabama, and we'd be moving at night, and you're moving from one grid square to the next, and you're with the student bozo platoon leader who has already taken you past this rock formation three times and doesn't recognize it."

He did this ten days on, a few days off, for a year: up before dawn, move his men to a new location, give them a series of missions to accomplish in a certain amount of time. Depending on the weather and the people he had, that could be to capture and secure a rocket site, or at least a rock that was designated the rocket site for purposes of training; dump something in a swamp and find it; overtake a pretend Vietcong stronghold; find a rice cache at a trail junction; or set up claymore mines.

But the actions were not the purpose. None of the exercises in themselves had any relevance to actual combat. The purpose was to form the habit of silence and ingrain it so that every soldier automatically thought that way. A quiet soldier was a live soldier, and Skip trained each of his men to be a very quiet soldier.

He was an excellent teacher: all his evaluations stated that he was extraordinary. But being so good landed him in trouble. The army has its ways of doing things and it sticks to them. As Skip taught more and more, he developed a more efficient style, which did not please the immediate higher command, who went by the book. He often was insubordinate to the captains and majors above him, to the point where they put him on report and wanted to demote him. To see whether that should be done, a colonel was sent on a night patrol with him. To make things more difficult, the colonel confiscated all compasses, which did not faze Skip; he simply did everything by the North Star. When they came back to the base, Skip overheard the major who advocated his demotion tell the colonel, "That bastard, he's insubordinate."

The colonel could not have cared less. "He's the best we've got," he said, and that was the end of the complaints.

"I was a cocky little bastard," Skip says now. "I could have done what I did with less attitude."

He preferred being out in the swamps and wilderness to being at Fort Benning, where he shared a bachelor pad with three other guys. He had the smallest room ("an expanded broom closet") because he originally was supposed to be trained as a mortar platoon leader and the extra time in training put him behind the rest of his class in finding housing, one of the reasons he found being in the field a better alternative. Even with better housing, though, it would not have been much different to him.

"On base at night, you spend your time just cleaning gear. The worst part of being in the military is being back on the base because it's the worst lowering of cultural standards in America. The army finds the lowest level—everything's blah. There's no engagement, no way for conversation. They just house you preliminary to getting you out to war."

After twenty-three years of relatively similar lives, it's hard to imagine how Skip and I could now have turned in directions more divergent. As he taught ambush and patrol and how to survive being shot at in the jungle, I considered my answers to the twenty-five questions and demands for information asked on Selective Service System Form No. 150 (Revised 2-9-59): Special Form for Conscientious Objector. I had my choice of two categories: (a) "I am, by reason of my religious training and belief, conscientiously opposed to participation in war of any form. I, therefore, claim exemption from combat training and service in the Armed Forces"; or (b) "I am, by reason of my religious training and belief, conscientiously opposed to participation in war of any form and I am further conscientiously opposed to participation in noncombatant training and service in the Armed Forces. I, therefore, claim exemption from both combatant and noncombatant training and service in the Armed Forces." I chose (b). This did not mean that I wanted relief from any obligation to the country. I was willing to do two years of nonmilitary national service, whether it had been the Peace Corps or, as was the case of a friend, emptying bedpans in a mental hospital. I didn't argue with the law that young men could be drafted by the government. I just objected to being part of the military in any way, because even as a noncombatant, I would be aiding in war.

The questions and information requested, "intended to obtain evidence of the genuineness of the claim," were specific and exhaustive: "Do you believe in a Supreme Being?" "Describe the nature of your belief which is the cause of your claim and state whether or not your belief in a Supreme Being involved duties which to you are superior to those arising from any human situation." "Explain how, when, and from whom or from what source you received the training and acquired the belief which is the basis of your claim. Give the name and present address of the individual upon whom you most rely for religious guidance." "Under what circumstances, if any, do you believe in the use of force?" "Describe the actions and behavior in your life which in your opinion most conspicuously demonstrate the consistency and depth of your religious convictions." "Have you ever given public expression, written or oral, to the views herein expressed as the basis for your claim?" "Are you a member of a religious sect or organization?" "If 'yes,' state the name of the sect, and the name and location of its governing body or head if known to you." "When, where, and how did you become a member of said sect or organization?" "State the name and location of the church, congregation, or meeting where you customarily attend." "Give the name, title, and present address of the pastor or leader of such church, congregation or meeting." "Describe carefully the creed or official statements of said religious sect or organization in relation to participation in war."

My responses ran to twenty-three typed pages and began:

> The essence of my belief is that Jesus Christ is the Son of God; that His teachings are that men should love rather than hate, to honor God, their common

Father; that all war and killing is in direct contradiction to God's way of redemptive love as revealed through Jesus Christ, and that inasmuch as Christ died for all men so, too, should I strive to follow Him and His "new commandment . . . that ye love one another as I have loved you, [for] by this shall men know ye are my disciples . . ." (John 13:34–35).

Moreover, Christ's teachings were summed up when He said, "You shall love the Lord your God with all your heart, and with all your soul, and with all your mind. This is the great and first commandment and the second is like it. You shall love your neighbor as yourself. There is no commandment greater than these" (Matthew 22:33–36, Mark 12:30–31).

I went on to aver that I could not sit passively and merely speak my belief, but that I had to show it actively in my life with the faith that evil cannot be overcome by evil, but by good alone. This included not participating with any armed force whose aim, however pacific, supports and employs violence in the resolution of conflicts. When a nation wages war, I added, it does so with the assumption that its ends are the right ones and that the killing will lead to a better tomorrow, though tomorrow's benefits are always doubtful and in the light of the new day do not seem quite what the fight was for. Certainty is ammunition for killing, I said. I quoted Oliver Cromwell's letter to the General Assembly of the Kirk of Scotland in August 1650, before the Battle of Dunbar against the Scots: "I beseech ye, in the bowels of Christ, think it possible ye may be mistaken," and I added, "It is unfortunate that Cromwell did not demand the same of himself." I wish I had then known Judge Learned Hand's testimony before a Senate committee in 1951 so I could have cited it as well: "I should like to have that written over the portals of every church, every school, and every court house, and, may I say, of every legislative body in the United States. I should like to have every court begin, 'I beseech ye in the bowels of Christ, think that ye may be mistaken.' "

I pointed out that pacifism was dominant for the first three centuries of the early Church: Justin Martyr, in 140, made it clear in his apology that Christians did not fight. Forty years later, Bishop (later Saint) Irenaeus expressed his conviction that Christians must not participate in war. About 200, Tertullian of Carthage pointed out in *De Corona Militia* the inconsistency of Christians bearing arms. Cyprian, the bishop of Carthage martyred in 258 in the Decian persecution, spoke for the Church then: "Christians are not allowed to kill; they must rather suffer death. . . . Christians must love their enemies, and it is the weapons of the spirit that they must use against their enemies." (Decius was Roman emperor only from 249–251, but in those two years he reverted to the almost abandoned paganism of ancient Rome and sought to eradicate Christianity. The persecution continued until 312 and the conversion of my would-be fraternity's inspiration, Constantine, who became the first Christian leader to countenance warfare.)

I credited my father with the bulk of my religious training and quoted from the catechism he taught me: "My duty to my neighbor is to love him as myself, and to do to all men as I would they should do unto me. . . . To hurt nobody by word or deed."

I divided force into two categories, violent and nonviolent. An example of the first is war; an example of the second is moral force. Christ practiced active nonviolence. When soldiers captured him on the Mount of Olives, one of the disciples, thought to be Simon Peter, cut off the ear of the high priest's slave, and the others asked, "Lord, shall we strike with the sword? . . . but Jesus answered, No more of this" (Luke 22:50–51). And I cited Gandhi: "Nonviolence is not passivity in any shape or form. It is the activist force in the world."

I approved of an unarmed police force on the order of Great Britain's and argued that violence and war are not necessities, but expedients. Humans are capable of behavioral extremes, from jungle behavior to high idealism. By accepting the jungle logic that war is inevitable, man denies his basic humanity, rather than exalts it.

I considered my membership in the Peace Corps as one public expression of my belief. Others were registering as a conscientious objector with the Episcopal Church through its registrar for COs in New York; membership in the Episcopal Peace Fellowship; and membership in the Fellowship of Reconciliation. For each of the latter two, I signed statements to work to discover and practice alternatives to violence and strive to build a social order.

As for the Episcopal Church's statements on participation, I quoted from a half dozen, among them the 1967 Resolution of Conscientious Objector recognizing its propriety, and the Pastoral Letter of 1939, which stated in part, "war as an instrument of national policy is a hideous denial of God and His condemnation rests upon it. It is rationally unjustifiable, morally indefensible, and religiously irreconcilable with the love of God and our neighbor."

"You've said it all," a Trust Territory government friend in Truk who supported me said, while chiding me for the length of my answers, "and then some."

One section of Form 150 asked for information on "persons who could supply information as to the sincerity of your professed convictions against participation in war." I sent a copy of my statement, along with a letter of explanation, to many people who had known me for years. I knew that draft boards tended to give more weight to testimonials from people who were not themselves conscientious objectors but who would say they believed I was and that my statement was consistent with what they had observed in my behavior. I cast a wide net and held my breath, not sure how some would react.

An early response came from the headmaster of San Miguel, who had arrived my junior year, a priest with slicked-back hair and a matching personality. I didn't much like him, but I felt he would be considered a good reference. I had last seen him six years before, when on graduation day he was all smiles and glowing words as he handed me the award given to the senior who supposedly most typified the values of the school. That was then. His curt letter said he certainly would not write anything on my behalf. Episcopalians could not be conscientious objectors, he (wrongly) informed me, adding that I was a disgrace to San Miguel and a coward, as well.

I braced myself for more letters like this, but his was the only rejection. Three Episcopal bishops, three Episcopal priests, a navy chaplain, a marine general, the Hobart dean, two Peace Corps staff members, a Trust Territory government official, Andy Connolly, and my parents were among those who wrote on my behalf. ("Even as a young boy, he was never interested in war games or war toys," my mother wrote. And she quoted from one of my letters: "My life, I hope, will be a life of action where I physically and spiritually work for peace on Earth, good will to men.") All said they were not pacifists but they were convinced of my sincerity and had seen it in my actions. I remember being touched and grateful (and still am, as well as a bit amazed) that so many people would attest so strongly to my character and my sense of faith.

My statement was completed and sent out in the first half of 1968, my last six months in Truk. To quickly recap that tumultuous time:

In January, North Vietnamese and Vietcong soldiers mount the Tet Offensive across most of South Vietnam. The brutal fighting over the next month produces devastating North Vietnamese losses but also erodes the support of Congress and average Americans for a war they now see as going on indefinitely. An American officer, referring to a small city near Saigon leveled by American bombs, finds his way into every future book of quotations when he says, "It became necessary to destroy the town to save it."

In February, Saigon police chief Nguyen Ngoc Loan is photographed by Eddie Adams and an NBC TV cameraman as he executes a handcuffed Vietcong officer point-blank with a pistol shot to the head. Former vice president Richard Nixon announces his candidacy for the Republican nomination for president. CBS TV news anchor Walter Cronkite, considered the most trusted man in America, tells his audience after a visit to Saigon that "the bloody experience of Vietnam is to end in a stalemate."

In March, public opinion polls after the Tet Offensive show that President Johnson's overall approval rating has slipped to 36 percent, while approval of his Vietnam War policy has dropped to 26 percent. He defeats antiwar Democrat Eugene McCarthy in the New Hampshire Democratic primary election by only three hundred votes. Senator Robert F. Kennedy announces his candidacy for the Democratic presidential nomination, and says of his participation in forming President John F. Kennedy's Vietnam policy, "past error is no excuse for its own perpetuation." In Vietnam, members of the First Battalion, Twentieth Infantry (American) Division, looking for suspected Vietcong encampments in Quang Ngai Province, enter the village of My Lai. Finding no Vietcong, they begin killing every civilian in sight, interrupted only by helicopter pilot Hugh Thompson, who lands and begins evacuating civilians after realizing what is happening. It will be a year before the massacre is made public. Antiwar students seize a building at Bowie State College in Maryland.

When Nelson Rockefeller looks like he is going to become a candidate for the Republican presidential nomination, my father makes clear he will not support him because he is divorced: "Any man who can't keep his marriage vows can't be president." (It struck me as ironic for a member of the Anglican Communion to feel this way, since the Church came to be because Henry VIII wanted a divorce.) In any event, I tell my father, "I could vote for Rockefeller but would like to know more on his stand on Vietnam. It would be great if McCarthy got the nomination away from Johnson, but that would be like General [Lewis B.] Hershey [the head of the Selective Service System] coming out in favor of draft resistors." Toward the end of the month, Rockefeller decides not to run. "You may be interested to know," I write home, "that with Rockefeller's refusal to run I am severing my affiliation with the Republican Party. Richard Nixon isn't my answer to anything. I can hardly wait to vote for McCarthy in the June primary. I think there really is a good chance to rid ourselves of Lyndon if only we will dedicate ourselves to it and start thinking again." A week later, Johnson announces that he will not seek reelection.

On April 2, Senator Eugene McCarthy wins the Democratic primary in Wisconsin. Two days later, the Reverend Martin Luther King, Jr., is assassinated by James Earl Ray in Memphis, Tennessee, at age thirty-nine. Racial unrest then erupts in more than one hundred American cities. Students seize the administration building at Ohio State University.

In May, peace talks begin in Paris between the United States and North Vietnam. The Poor People's March, led by the Reverend Ralph Abernathy, King's replacement as head of the Southern Christian Leadership Conference, reaches Washington, D.C. The Czechoslovakian government announces liberalizing reforms under Alexander Dubček. Eugene McCarthy wins the Democratic primary in Oregon.

In June, Daniel Ellsberg is indicted for leaking the Pentagon Papers, the detailed account of American government and military duplicity in Vietnam. Robert F. Kennedy is shot by Sirhan Sirhan in the Ambassador Hotel in Los Angeles, and dies the next day. The news comes by radio to Tsis, completely confusing and horrifying the locals, who ask me why this happened. I shinny up a coconut palm and try to gather myself in order to think of some sort of explanation, without success.

A s my Peace Corps service drew to an end, I was required to take a physical. It included a PPD skin test for tuberculosis. The hard, raised red reaction around the injection site was three times what was normal, clear evidence that I had been exposed to TB, which was not a surprise, considering many of the Trukese had it to one degree or another, especially those in Tsis's part of the lagoon. Fortunately, a chest X-ray showed no evidence of it, but when the retest was even more positive, I was given a bottle of one thousand Isoniazid (INH) tablets and instructed to take three a day for a year; the PPD reaction showed that the TB germ had been trapped by my immune system before it could make me ill, but the medication was necessary to make sure that stayed the case. The one upside to this, I wrote my parents, was that I likely would have a medical deferment from the draft board while I was on the medication. Still, I wasn't at all confident about the long term: "Do they have TB wards in prisons?"

In July, I left Truk. I felt some sadness about going and some regret that I had not done more to help the islanders, but more than anything, I felt relief. I was glad for the experience and glad it was over. I had adapted to Trukese life but would never adopt it; I had another life to return to. A bunch of folks from Tsis came to Moen in a downpour to see me off, decorating me with *mwárámwárs* and leis. They thought I was leaving but I knew I was escaping, and I felt guilty for that and because none of them ever would. Instead, the "progress" that I had been so much a part of would likely erode the old culture and bring nothing better in return. The jet age had recently come to Micronesia, and what had been a three-hour trip to Guam now took forty-five minutes. I'd be there and into another world before they got back to Tsis.

With a Peace Corps buddy I began a westward trip home through Asia, the Middle East, and Europe, flying on a ticket from Pan American World Airways that cost $900 and allowed for unlimited stops so long as we continued in the same direction. Every volunteer had $75 a month banked for them by the Peace Corps as a "readjustment allowance," which we used to pay our way, but readjustment turned out to require more than money. In Calcutta we read in the *International Herald Tribune* about a three-day race riot in Gary, Indiana. We were in Rome when the news came that Warsaw Pact forces had entered Czechoslovakia to end the reform movement that had flowered that summer, and in Florence when the Democratic Convention opened in Chicago six days later. We listened to it unfold on the radio in disbelief and disgust as the antiwar demonstrators in Grant Park were tear-gassed and beaten by the police, and sympathetic delegates to the convention were shouted down by Mayor Richard Daley and others. To two young men who had been barefoot for two years on tiny islands in a time warp, the world was unrecogniz- able even though we knew a lot of the news. But seen for so long from many thousands of miles away was far differ- ent than being suddenly in the milieu. By the time we reached England, I was fearful of returning to the United States. Assassinations, race riots, antiwar demonstrations, police beatings, and the Czech crackdown combined to make me feel that an antiwar pacifist peacenik such as I would not be welcome at home. Though I know the feel- ing was irrational, I was deeply worried that as soon as I returned, I would be arrested on some specious charge. I was trembling when I went through customs at Kennedy Airport in New York—without incident.

T he culture shock I felt in my first weeks on Tsis struck a reverse whammy in America. I found myself trapped between two worlds. I couldn't go into a supermarket; there were too many choices. After living with people who often had only one meal a day, there was too much food, not only in the markets but everywhere. Television was too fast, the shows superficial, the commercials inane. Before going to California, I stopped in Washington, D.C., to interview for a position as a Peace Corps Fellow, one of a dozen volunteers chosen each year to spend a year working in various jobs at headquarters in preparation for leading a program overseas. I was accepted, with a starting salary of $8,500, only slightly less than my father was then making, if you included free use of the rectory. The first couple of days at home after two years away were a difficult readjustment of their own as I put aside the independence I was used to and became a son again. I had let my hair grow fashionably long on the trip home (that is to say, about two inches), though it turned out that long hair was not yet fashionable in El Cajon. Among the first words my father said after we reunited at the airport were, "When are you going to get it cut?" It was one of the few times in my life he disappointed me, and once alone in my room I cried. He and our doctor friend had recently come to a personal truce, though not a theological one; the doctor continued to attend a Catholic church and his views on race had not much mediated, but he hosted a lovely welcome-home dinner in a fancy restaurant. A few days later, I was sent to be checked out by him, in part to see if there were any signs of TB. We had a pleasant chat; then as he examined me, he said, "I assume you're integrated."

"I guess so," I replied, not sure what he meant, but thinking that he presumed I supported racial equality. Only much later did I realize he was asking if I'd had sex with a Trukese woman.

In September, I wrote to my draft board to tell them that I would be living and working in Washington, and I requested that they continue my 2-A classification now that I was a Peace Corps Fellow, though I figured with the esclation of the war there would be a fight. In late

October, I began my job in the Peace Corps headquarters, across Lafayette Square from the White House, into which Richard Nixon would move the following January. The same week, my draft board responded to my request with a form letter. I was now classified 1-A.

Six

W
hat would turn out to be the most important
news for Skip in July 1968, shortly before his
deployment to Vietnam, was the replacement
of Gen. William Westmoreland by Gen. Creighton Abrams
as commander of the American troops in the war. Westmoreland favored company-strength sweeps through the
countryside and jungle, which often left soldiers exposed
as they searched for the Vietcong. But just as Skip arrived
as a member of the First Infantry Division after his year of
teaching ambush and patrol, the emphasis, to his amaze-
ment, shifted to Abrams's "hide and wait" philosophy.

"How did I know they were going to change the manner
of warfare in Vietnam while I was on the plane to ambushing and patrolling, the very thing I had been doing for a
year?" he marveled decades later. "The wave shifted and I
caught it. When General Westmoreland was there, they
would do some of this foolishness of sweeping on-line

through the jungle that was like taking a pie tin to roust a tiger in the bush. Some part of the line would encounter a base camp and all hell would break loose. General Abrams got the idea, 'Hey, why don't we set up ambush patrols and let them come to us?' Douglas MacArthur used a variation of this tactic on a grander scale in the Pacific. It chokes off their supplies. They have to come out for rice and stuff. And if the other guy makes the mistake of breaking light and sound before you do, he's toast."

In this zero-sum reality of kill or be killed, Lieutenant Packard thought like an instructor. When he arrived, he realized his men needed retraining: Rather than keeping themselves covered, they would stroll down the trail; they did not strong-point—find a location that by its site and nature could easily be defended; they weren't camouflaging.

"They weren't being jungle fighters," he recalled. "They were being Snuffies."

To his troops' initial puzzlement about why all this was necessary, Skip took them outside the perimeter of the camp and made them repeat and repeat and repeat what he'd taught at Fort Benning, showing them precisely how to keep a low profile to protect themselves on the trail from a surprise attack, how to hide and how to keep quiet. He trained them to shoot at the feet of an enemy and slightly off the closest side of the trail, because at the first shot, his enemy's instinct would be to dive into the brush for cover, and aiming low allowed for the rifle's recoil that raised the barrel. He quickly molded his men into a cohesive group, knowing this would make all of them safer.

"People think of the war in terms of how they're trained," he said years later. "The army spent eight weeks in basic training and then eight weeks more indoctrinating you and getting you to connect and bond with a group and be cohesive. Then you left those people and went in onesies and twosies to Vietnam, and either you bonded quickly with those new guys and were better off, or you didn't and were headed for trouble. I bonded with them. They liked being around me. And I liked being around them." They had another good reason to like the lieutenant. They realized he knew how to keep them alive.

Among the skills he taught was to lay a claymore mine properly. A claymore (named after the large two-handed medieval Scottish sword) is about eight inches long, one and a half inches wide, and five inches high. Convex in front and concave in back, it blasts out seven hundred pieces of steel-ball shrapnel 150 feet in an arc of sixty degrees. As it is designed to explode forward, one side of the mine is embossed FRONT, and below that, TOWARD ENEMY, but in the adrenaline rush to lay them, a soldier, especially a new one, doesn't always read the directions. A claymore can be detonated by an electrical charge, by a timer, or by a trip wire.

Even with so much practice, and his toughness with his men, Skip's first ambush was nothing, of course, like training. Whenever possible, the officer in charge is first taken by helicopter to survey the area where he and his men will be deployed. Maps are covered with a grid and he notes the coordinates while in the air, so if artillery support is needed, he'll know where to direct it. Skip was taken up and made appropriate notes in the small black-covered copy of the New Testament he always carried. Anything made of paper quickly became dog-eared and wet if it wasn't wrapped in cellophane, which is how Skip protected his book. He always kept it on him "for sentiment. If I was going to buy it, I wanted to have stuff on me that looked respectable." And he carried it because soldiers in combat are superstitious. Similarly, for no particular reason, before Skip's first ambush he tied a piece of parachute cord around his neck. He didn't die, so he kept it on for months. (Most soldiers who died in Vietnam did so in their first three months.)

In the argot of the army, to carry out an ambush is to "blow it." The kill zone is where the bodies are. After Skip and his men blew their first ambush, he went out into the kill zone with his men to count the enemy dead and drag them into the bush and off the trail so other Vietcong would not easily find them and know they had been detected. It was a grisly sight. Claymores are not subtle in their damage. They send body parts flying, and in the backwash of the explosion, blood and pieces of flesh commonly land on those who set the mine.

"Igniting them upon the enemy," Skip says, "is like entering hell."

As he looked upon those who had just died, the acolyte soldier tried to say a prayer, to isolate the moment for more than tabulating a body count. Okay, he thought, this is the time that you break down and have a psychic insight. But it was not as clear as that. His first reaction to the mangled bodies was no reaction. He had, he said, a "sort of

spiritually choking feeling, like I was drained of any emotion. I know now because I've seen a lot of shrinks; it's
what you call 'numbing.' Nowadays my expert friends tell
me I was in post-traumatic stress. One of my platoon ser-
geants to this day swears that I was reading the New Testament over the bodies. Actually, I was checking the grid
coordinates that I had put in my little black New Testament, but I can't convince him."

Skip quickly realized that not only was he good at what
he did; he was better than most, and part of him took
pride in his efficiency. "The army trains you to do extraordinary things under fire," he says, and he liked carrying out
his task, the habits of ambush and patrol guiding him,
rather than the habits he was brought up with. His worldview was turned upside down. Killing was the norm, what
kept one alive. He was methodical, he says, not brave:
"There is little bravery on the battlefield. Mostly it's reflex
to training." Nor is there room for compassion for those
who would kill you. Ambushing requires constantly moving on and demands there can be no prisoners taken nor
wounded left on the field to give away your position,
because often other patrols are nearby.

"When a claymore blows your stomach to another part
of the trail junction, trying to put that stomach back
doesn't work," he says now. "And we had to keep moving."

Moreover, bodies had to be searched for any bits of
intelligence, and any identification destroyed, so that if or
when other Vietcong came upon them, they would not
know the units the men belonged to. Soldiers on each side
took useful equipment off the dead. Skip gathered up

photos of girlfriends and family from the bodies, because they could provide identifying information of troop movement to cohorts who came upon the dead. On one he found a picture of a blond woman that had likely been taken from an American the soldier had killed. Out of sight of his men, Skip burned the photos, lives as well as identities extinguished. He felt that he held something precious that he had taken away from the dead along with their lives. He has often wished since that he could apologize to their families. He still sees in his mind some of the wounded before they were killed, and the recollection of all that was required of him and his men that they did with such single-mindedness and success makes him dizzy when he recounts it and disrupts his equilibrium and sleep.

He says, "My personality has been changed and in some way I worry if it's been mottled, if I'm odd in that way. Other people didn't do this stuff—they're civilized; they didn't do this stuff. It's hard. This is something I carry with me all the time. I have nightmares that I haven't done something, that I didn't finish burying someone. Why was it necessary to kill these people? It's just shitty; it's *awful*."

In his first months in Vietnam, however, he was totally focused on carrying out his mission. His obsessive-compulsive disorder, he says, "made light and sound important. Claymore mines had to be positioned in a certain way. You had to enter a site a certain way, and if we didn't, I made us go back out again. You've seen *Monk*? [A television series about an obsessive-compulsive detective.] I was medicated for the disorder when I came back, so it's gotten progressively better."

It was not until the stress of Vietnam that Skip's until then minor obsessive-compulsiveness grew more intense and overtly exhibited itself, and it worked to his benefit in the jungle. He says when he "had anxiety, I bound into those habits fast. They saved my life. I'd always crawl out to make sure claymores were pointed the right way, because sometimes these yo-yos would have put them the wrong way. I'd crawl over the guys to make sure everybody had chambered a round ahead of time—it makes a sound like clicking a pen and you don't want to be doing it when the enemy is approaching you in the stillness. Some operations you'd want to chamber a round but sometimes not, because of noncombatants in the area."

In the Vietnam War, the face of a platoon changed every month or six weeks as men rotated in and out, which was a problem for a lieutenant trying to maintain a highly trained and disciplined group for ambush and patrol. In a piece of good fortune, Skip was able to keep his medic, David Rogers, for his last three months leading the platoon. Rogers was a conscientious objector with noncombatant status (1-AO) who served but carried no weapon. Twenty-two and thus straight in the sights of the Selective Service System, he accepted that he was "born to be drafted." He had been raised a Roman Catholic, but his father became a Quaker and pacifism rubbed off on him. On the other hand, there were many young men from his town in the war to whom he felt a kind of kinship. A photograph in *Time* or *Life* of a medic treating wounded marines in Hue during the Tet Offensive in 1968 made him feel that this was a middle ground he could take. His choice was made more difficult when his father, hopeful that David would face prison rather than be drafted, told him "in no uncertain terms that I was selling out" by being an unarmed medic, though his father did come to accept the choice. The two eventually reconciled but it was a difficult time for Rogers, who still feels "there weren't any good answers regarding the war and killing."

The lieutenant and his medic, each with a mordant sense of humor and an aura of cool, immediately clicked. Rogers called his lieutenant "3–6," his radio call sign (all sixes were platoon leaders; theirs was the third platoon). Three-six called his medic "Doc." They still do.

Most soldiers in Vietnam were just out of high school, and to try to stabilize the platoon, the lieutenant and the medic looked for a particular kind of soldier, someone, Skip said, with "some inner core, some maturity. I didn't want someone who was gung ho. I didn't need anybody like that, who was only going to get me into trouble." When new men arrived, Rogers would use his position as medic to examine their feet, a ruse to enter into casual conversation. When Rogers found a good fit, he gave Skip a signal. "It wasn't Carol Burnett–like, where he pulled his earlobe, but something like that, very sophomoric. Then I would say to the first sergeant, 'I want Smith, Jones.' When asked why, I'd say, 'I just think he'll fit in.' David was very savvy. It wasn't a Studs Terkel conversation, but just while checking a guy's feet and talking, he could spot who'd be good for ambush and patrol."

Being good required developing what in many ways was an alternative personality, Skip later explained to me. "It takes time to develop a habit that you won't use in 'the

world'—that's what they call where we are today. The
other was 'Vietnam.' You have to develop that habit and
maybe seventy others. You have to lie on the ground, shit
in public, make sure that you're ready to kill somebody—
all kinds of things that aren't natural."

For the most part, the only times he had "a sense of oth-
erness, a spooky sense of ominous presence, was when it
was night and quiet," he told me. "When you're on a mission, you're doing only one thing. You're thinking only of
how they are pursuing you. These were hard-core Viet
cong soldiers and occasionally Chinese mercenaries, and
when we would touch down, they knew it was us and they
would track us. Ambush and patrol platoons carried out
many missions over time in the same large area, and a certain familiarity grew between us, or at least a familiarity
with tactics. So it got to the point where I would stay
behind to set an ambush on them. I wanted the soldier I
positioned there to kill the enemy scout, who I guessed
was following me. Sometimes I'd think when I left the kid
behind that I wouldn't see him again because there was
a good chance the Vietcong who were tracking us were a
lot better than our guys. Then the VC got wise to what
I was doing. But that was the kind of high alert I was
always on."

These were not things one wrote home about. Skip had
no idea how to describe to me what he was doing, and so
he didn't. He did a bit to his wife, but, he says, his accounts
scared her. When she flew to Honolulu to meet him on his
rest and recreation break, he says she was unsure of who
the man would be, and even whether she would be safe

Lieutenant Packard (right foreground)
and platoon on patrol, 1969

with him. The visit reunited them, and for Skip, being in a loving situation rather than a killing one, briefly undid him. One night after a couple of drinks, he started to cry uncontrollably. Thirty-six hours later, he was back in Vietnam, flying in a beelike helicopter that dropped him into his platoon literally in the middle of an operation. Did I dream that I was in Hawaii? he asked himself.

It is comforting to think there are civilizing curbs and rules to battle, but there is nothing civilized about ending another person's life, and at close range. The emotional price paid by soldiers and the trauma inflicted on them by killing and killing again is steep. "Bringing someone off that," Skip says now, "is very hard to do."

Everyone on the battlefield is a participant, even unarmed conscientious objectors serving as medics. "You were part of the platoon," David Rogers recalls. "After Three-six left the platoon, I stayed with it in the field for five or six months more. Over time, I became one of the most experienced guys. I wasn't calling in fire but when they were trying to pick an ambush site or where to go, there were times people asked me what I thought. You couldn't keep yourself separate. I've had to live with that ever since. We killed twelve people one night and a thirteenth in the morning. More often the numbers were smaller. We were always counting and there was a balance to it all. Walking away with the blood on the grass I would always think that the next time it would be one of us.

"After fighting we would search the bodies and that made it more personal. It wasn't a matter of taking trophies. It was gear that was useful. When the rains were beginning to let up, I left my poncho behind for a lighter one we got from an enemy soldier. We found a medical journal that I kept because I admired the detail of the drawings by the medic on the other side. And one night there was a picture of a child with a drawing of a dove on the back. I have kept that in my Bible ever since."

Like Skip, Rogers continues to pay a price for his service. "I have a dream that I am in a bookstore leafing through a book about the war by a North Vietnamese soldier. He is telling details about the stuff I carried, and I realize I am dead and he has searched my body. After I came home, for many years I didn't think it was right to take Communion. The first time I did was when my mother died in 1993. You never really get over it, and I always think of that Old Testament passage [I Chronicles 28:3] where God tells David that he wants Solomon to build the temple, because there's too much blood on David's hands."

Skip tried to layer in bits of "the world" to his daily life.

One was attending church services in the field. There was an Episcopal chaplain for the battalion of four or five companies—with four platoons to a company—who traveled with them on maneuvers, which was unusual. He even went on a couple of patrols, "but not with my platoon," Skip recalled. "He made too much noise, so I just made sure he stayed behind." On Sundays, the chaplain held services in the mess tent, and for Skip, kneeling on bare ground in the tent and participating in the recitation of prayers was "like a memory of home, though the services were bizarre on one level, as they weren't integrated with where we were. Religion in the army is not like it was at Hobart. You went because—you went."

Besides David Rogers, Skip had a close friendship with Capt. Chester Davis, his company commander and a practicing Episcopalian. "We hit it off because we were odd, kindred souls in the battalion. He was more of an intellectual than most and was wounded during his first tour in Vietnam. His wound disfigured him: The bullet traveled up his arm and exited out the elbow. He wangled staying in the army by teaching at Fort Benning and further wangled his way back to Nam. As for me, I may have taught the Rangers back at Fort Benning, but the grizzled command didn't trust me because I was a wiseass. As it would turn out, he and I were awarded the Silver Star at the same ceremony for different engagements; it was his second one."

Davis, obviously an excellent soldier, saw firsthand how good Skip was. He listened on the radio as Skip's platoon met a larger number of Vietcong who surprised and tried to overrun them. Skip engaged his men in such a way that they all survived and it was the Vietcong who were killed.

He was awarded a Bronze Star with a *V* (for valor) device and an oak-leaf cluster for how he led his men. (He received another Bronze Star with a *V* device and cluster but does not remember for which battle, "because there were so many.")

In the aftermath of the bloodshed and disposal of the bodies and the adrenaline rush that helped them perform so well in a savage situation, the two friends sought a connection with normalcy. "Our conversation included how we would invite an Episcopal chaplain we knew to our base camp for a celebration of Holy Communion," Skip recalls. "I know I am reaching back in judgment with this thought now, but I am struck by how layered my practiced churchmanship was from the very gruesome deeds I had just done." That practiced churchmanship, however, kept alive the notion that perhaps he would go to seminary after the army was done with him.

Getting from dawn to dusk, from dusk to dawn, from day to day, was made easier, Skip says, by habits and ceremonies. "During the rainy season, being out in the bush was hard, so Captain Davis theorized that you could survive anything if you brought your 'comfort index' down to a manageable—but no lower—level. He showed me how to make cocoa with C rations. He was very particular about it: one packet of cocoa in an emptied tin, stirred continuously as you poured in water and artificial creamer. The art was to avoid clots. Creating the stirrer was a fetish, too—it had to be whittled from a twig, but not just any twig; it had to be green. I really looked forward to those times, and yet when I look back on them now, it makes me wince. Our cocoa parties would happen not many meters away from where I had obsessively arranged a brocade of claymore mines."

I wrote to Skip every few weeks or so, as I had from Truk, trying to amuse a friend in what I knew were unamusing conditions, though I never imagined they were so brutal. I passed on whatever news of friends I had, and kept him posted on my quest for CO status. He wrote far less often than I (he ended one letter, "Whatever you do, stay out of the Army"), and when he did, he offered no accounts of what he was doing, for the reasons that he later made clear. Now, having learned how fraught with danger his time there was, a letter that arrived in July 1969, after my girlfriend (who was friendly with Skip from college) and I sent him a boxful of silly things, amazes me with its lightheartedness.

> Dear Eric and Janee,
> I received your goodies box, goodies is an
> understatement, they were a windfall. Two [South]
> Vietnamese seized the airplane, and made off with
> it and promptly flew it into a bamboo thicket.
> Simultaneously, everyone began recalling how they
> "used to be pretty good with a yo-yo." After 40
> variations of "around-the-world" I was able to parry
> the group off into some jacks competition. The ever-
> present heat rendered the chocolate chips into one
> glutinous mass—we sliced it up like a limp salmon,
> still goo, we left it in the wrapper during surgery.
> The Play-Doh fell on . . . dead hands—each

squeezed, smiled, and passed it on. I tried to
expound the virtues of creativeness by burrowing
my thumb into it, getting a blue fingernail and some
turned backs. I tried. I kept order with the laser (or
disorder).

I'm concerned about your alternate service.
I'm advised by my medic [Rogers] that your C.O.
status *won't* bring you in or near olive drab. Thank
God. My medic is a C.O., who when he got his
C.O. status approved, whammo, along came Uncle
Sam. He's a 1-AO, or a C.O. with non-combatant
status, hence he's a medic with no weapon. You
hopefully will have a 1-O allowing an alternative
civilian service. The fact that the Peace Corps
doesn't fit that category at least partially is
disgusting. My RTO [radiotelephone operator]
spent two years in the Peace Corps swatting flies
in the Brazilian jungle for freedom, brotherhood,
and country (either one). Now what's he doing?
Why he's swatting flies in the Vietnamese jungle
for freedom. . . .

P.S. Send me a couple more yo-yos.

"I'd read your letters to the platoon," he told me many
years later. "There were letters from two people we would
read. David Rogers would read letters from Harry, a
friend from college. And yours."

I wondered how that seemed, hearing from someone
who had no one shooting at him. Did the letters evoke

envy that I was safe? Or derision because I was fighting the draft? The answer was neither.

"When you're in an ambush site during the daylight, you can relax. I'd let people light up for smokes. It's at night when you have to be careful. I'd say, 'I have another letter from Eric.' They'd get some sticks and be stirring their cocoa with them. It was like, here's a letter from the South Seas. There wasn't any kind of envy or derision. It was being distracted.

"There was a disconnection between social conversation and what was going on in the jungle. There's a sense of living in another world. A lot of being in the military is making it through, one daylight to one dusk, one dusk to one daylight. When you're short-time and close to your departure date, everybody's counting their days. Everything else—you, my wife, my family—is kind of not relevant. The only people relevant to me are the people covering my ass. So it's a bit of a luxury envying Eric, who made the right choice."

My 1-A draft classification hung over me for more than a year. Shortly after I received it in the fall of 1968, a letter arrived in El Cajon, ordering me to report for a physical in Los Angeles. Because I lived and worked in Washington, the rules allowed me to request that the physical be transferred, a process that could take months. At the same time, I continued to pursue my CO status, and because there were so many letters, forms, and other filings for both my 1-O application and the transfer for the physical, on several occasions I asked my father to go to the draft-board office to be sure all was there. In February 1969, he reported on one of those visits:

O fragile thread, upon which hangs the future of America:

I went down to the draft board as you requested yesterday to review your file once more. They know me there; they smile at me; they offer me seats; they say "Good Morning, Rev."; they move me to the counter. I am so much a fixture there that a typist, coming in from her coffee break, tried to hang her coat on me. She had a mean look. Had I been 20 years younger, I am sure her coat would not be the only thing she would try to hang on me.

They don't put your file away any more; they just reach under the counter for it, after I say, through the corner of my mouth, "Eric sent me." It is a nice file. There is a spot on the top left corner on the inside, and two slight tears where they have removed the report of the Truk Doctor, and sent it to Los Angeles with the papers for your physical. It is getting a little dog-eared from frequent usage, and the little blue tag is beginning to look the worse for wear, but otherwise it is a typical Lax file—a little questionable and bulging at the seams. . . .

Oh yes. The letter is there, written or dated Nov. 1st and word for word as you directed it would be over the phone.

P.S. Any time. I was just beginning to make time with Grandma Moses at the first desk, and it's a shame to let it drop, now.

Eventually, a notice arrived, ordering me to report at 6:00 a.m. on a late May morning to the District of Columbia draft-board office, from which I'd be taken to a physical at Fort Holabird, in Baltimore. Men had to register for the draft at eighteen and were eligible until their twenty-sixth birthday. I had just turned twenty-four when I left Truk in July 1968. There were then more than 500,000 troops in Vietnam, an increase of 150,000 in two years, and anyone with a 1-A classification was likely to be drafted, provided he passed the army physical. People did all sorts of things in an attempt to flunk it. They stayed up for days, took a variety of stimulants, or showed up drunk. They tried to fail the hearing test; they told doctors they were bed wetters; they feigned homosexuality; they came with letters from physicians who attested to one bodily failure or another. I briefly considered such evasive action but decided against it. The draft and I were going to duke it out, winner take all. I showed up on the appointed morning, and, as I wrote to a friend afterward,

> we all piled on buses while some of the local
> resistance handed out leaflets that informed us "You
> don't gotta go" and advised us "Don't sign the loyalty
> oath," as that will delay induction 30 to 60 days or
> even permanently. Just as we were ready to leave, a
> stern Southern captain got on the bus and told us
> that some of us were going for induction and would
> be at Fort Bragg, North Carolina, by nightfall, while
> those going for physicals would be back around four,
> if we cooperated. Then a black guy in the back of the
> bus asked if we were supposed to have checked in
> before we got on the bus, and the captain said yes,

but he'd be glad to do it for him, but the black guy said, "Uhuh, I'll do it, it's probably the last thing I'll be able to decide for myself for two years," and thereupon he pushed past the captain and out of the bus. We applauded.

Fort Holabird is a dingy place. [It was closed in 1973.] The buildings used for processing and physicals are old, and hot. We were sent to a small room and told that those of us with last names beginning with the letters A through L would stand on the left, M through Z on the right. That took ten minutes, as some people had trouble figuring out which line they were supposed to be in. We were given forms already filled in with our names and other pertinent data and a pencil and sent to another room. We sat at desks and then Sergeant Carusoe and Captain Fink walked in, followed by Privates Moog, Baker, and (I think) Dickson. Sgt. Carusoe called us "gentlemen" and explained that we were going to be in this hot room for a couple of hours, so why not open the windows and then listen to him? We filled out forms, which asked for a listing of all our run-ins with the police, ranging from minor traffic violations upward. One guy near me took a page and a half to list his. He also received an ovation when the private who checked the forms to see if we had a criminal record did the greatest double-take I've ever seen.

After our moral character was thus examined, we filled in whether we were white or black, how long

ERIC LAX

we had gone to school, and other similar stuff. Then
we got to take the mental test. It lasted 50 minutes
and had such questions as: "John bought his lunch.
A sandwich cost 25 cents, milk 15 cents, and dessert
10 cents. How much did John pay for lunch?" There
was a section on visual perception, where we
were shown a picture of a cube or other three-
dimensional figure, and then four choices of how
it looked unfolded. There were shaded squares and
squares with arrows and the like. Some of those
I found difficult. Then there was the reverse: an
unfolded figure and you had to decide which of four
choices it looked like folded up. The vocabulary
section was full of such words as "keen" and
"directive." There was a section showing a tool or a
mechanical part, and four choices of which tool or
mechanical part went with the one shown. I
probably did as well on that as the mechanically
inclined did on the vocabulary.

After the mental tests the medics came in, led by
a nasty and overgrown juvenile delinquent who
delighted in threatening us: "We can stay here all day
if you don't shut up, people. We can keep you here
up to 72 hours. It's up to you." He was all screwed
up in giving directions on how to fill out forms but
he wouldn't repeat anything, saying after someone
asked, "Tough. If the bastards don't get it right the
first time, too bad."

Finally we got down our medical histories and
then Private Moog came in with the mental test
results and lo and behold, 62 out of 120 had either

failed or so minimally passed that they were going
to have to take a couple of hours' more tests in the
afternoon. They went off first to get their physicals
so we could all leave together on the buses. Sgt.
Carusoe went off to cash a check, which infuriated
Pvt. Moog because he was left with only Pvt. Baker
to keep us under control.

Then the real fun began. We surrounded Moog
and Baker and pantsed them. Actually, we went
outside and waited. Eventually we were led to
another shed and told to take off our clothes, save
for our underwear and shoes. In small groups we
bent over and in moving unity spread our cheeks so
the doctors could check for dirty butts, or whatever.
Then a hernia check. If I had one, it would never
have been found. The doctor had come and gone
before I could either turn my head or cough. After
that, a blood pressure check, urination in a cup, a
chest X-ray, height and weight measurements, a
blood test, and a vision exam administered by a
harried Filipino.

Lunch was a boxed affair between two barracks.
Then the worst of all, waiting for an hour in a
cramped building overheated from the sun and dank
with the sweat of us all, to take a hearing test.
Finally, 10 of us walked into something like a vault
or walk-in freezer, which all the time I waited I
assumed was air-conditioned. It wasn't, and the
moment the door slammed shut, all fresh air
vanished. For the next 10 minutes I desperately tried
to distinguish between the ringing in my ears and

the faint sounds coming through the headphones, because if you screwed up, you were sent to the end of the line to take it again. I nearly fainted from the heat.

And then we were on our way to the doctor. A lot of guys had letters stating why they should be medically deferred but I doubt any were read, as the average time a doctor spent with one of us was about two minutes. Except for me. Mine turned out to have wanted to go to Micronesia with the Public Health Service and he asked me questions about the place for 45 minutes.

"Oh," he said at the end, as he glanced at my form, "you're taking INH"—it clearly showed that I had only one week more of the pills to go. "We can't take you until you're off these meds." And he deferred me for six months.

Guardian angels take on all sorts of outward appearances.

The bus ride back: Behind me, two stockbrokers; in front, a fellow freshly returned from the People's Park [in Berkeley, California, site of a riot between police, students, and antiwar demonstrators in May 1969] and a young Washington radical whose every utterance made it clear that he was full of yak shit. I got to the office at 4:30, as tired and withered as I ever hope to be.

I failed a second physical on another fluke and was deferred for six months more. (My blood pressure was a little high, no doubt from the anxiety that comes with an army physical. Had the doctor taken it a second time, as my own physician always did after my initial "white-coat syndrome" raised it, I'd probably have been within the acceptable range.) Meanwhile, I continued to press for my CO status. Anyone who disputed his draft classification could request a hearing before the board to make his case, and I asked for one. When it was accepted, I asked that it be transferred to Washington, and orders came for me to appear at 6:00 p.m. in the basement of a federal building not far from the Peace Corps headquarters. I waited to be called, alone on a bench in a quiet, dimly lighted hallway. After fifteen minutes or so, I heard footsteps, and then a black man in his fifties, wearing plain dark green clothes that at first glance made him look like a janitor, rounded the corner on my right and stopped by me.

"Hi, Eric," he said. I had never seen him in my life, but I said hello in return.

"What are you doing here?"

Waiting for a hearing on my application for conscientious objector status, I explained, and told him a bit about it after he asked. He listened attentively, then nodded his head when I'd finished.

"I've read it," he said. "You'll never leave Washington." And then he walked around the corner to my left. The only things in the building seemed to be me and the dying echoes of his footfalls. I was more than a bit spooked. How did he know my name? Did "You'll never leave Washington" mean I'd get my CO status, or be in prison here? And how did *he* know?

Presently I was called before the board of three men who would consider my case. One was an Episcopalian, who said Episcopalians could not qualify as COs. I politely corrected him and said where he could find proof in my statement. It was clear that none of them had read it. They asked many of the same questions I had answered in my statement and often challenged my responses. I held firm and detailed what I had written, and why. I made copious mental notes as this went on, which I wrote down immediately after I left the hearing room; their omissions and misunderstandings would be relevant for an appeal if necessary. After an hour, we were done. On my way out, I described the man who had spoken with me and asked if anyone knew who he was. They all did. He was an army lieutenant general, the head of the D.C. Selective Service. Obviously, he had come by to size me up.

Here's how I size myself up today: My earnestness in declaring myself a CO was, I think, evident to almost everyone I talked with about it. But in retrospect, it seems that over the years of arguing with my draft board, my earnestness blocked out in me the larger view of what being a conscientious objector represented, and that was keeping my faith at the forefront.

A crisis or serious worry often makes us turn to God, as I did when I made my decision not to fight. But how much of that decision was true faith, and how much was expediency? My easily held and unexamined belief during my childhood and first years in college was tested by the possibility of my being drafted to fight in Vietnam. I certainly did not want to fight in what seemed a senseless conflict and I was eager to find whatever legal deferment I could. The Peace Corps served two needs: It was a chance to be of service, something I firmly believed in, and it was a two-year deferment. Would I have joined the Peace Corps if there had been no Vietnam? As I had no burning academic aspirations and was unsure of what I wanted to make of my life, I'm confident I would have. It was a lucky opportunity; I can't think of anything else I'd rather have done or that was better suited to me.

But Vietnam was a consideration in the plans of every male who graduated when I did, and so the choices we all made had to be practical. I did believe in nonviolence, the effectiveness of which I saw in the gains Dr. King had made by it. I did believe the teachings of Jesus Christ are based on love and forgiveness. And so for the first time I found myself standing up for my faith because I had thought through what I believed, not just because it was what I had always done by rote. It is true that I wanted to do everything possible to stay out of a position where someone was shooting at me or I at them. But it also is true that I believed killing begets killing and that I was willing to accept the consequences and be sent to prison if my draft board didn't accept my position. In this instance, my conscience really was my guide.

I have often wondered what I would have done in World War II, which was fought for much clearer reasons and against clear evil. Certainly the three draft-board interviewers asked me what I would have done. The answer I gave them is still the best answer I've been able to find: I don't know. Under the law and, I think, in life, we are responsible only for the choices before us and how we behave, not how we might have. I made my choice based on what confronted me and acted according to my belief.

My draft saga, which had dragged on for over four years, ended quickly and without the confrontation between me and my draft board that could send me to prison. In the fall of 1969, I received my 1-O and I rejoiced; four years of anxiety and apprehension were over. I began the search for service that would be acceptable were I called, but only a few weeks later, on December 1, 1969, the first National Draft Lottery since 1942 was conducted. Those with a low number would be drafted. Those with a high one would not. Mine was 313, well out of range. And I wouldn't have to face next year's lottery because, in six months, I would turn twenty-six and no longer be draft-eligible.

I had never prayed that I be granted CO status and I didn't give a prayer of thanks that it came; both seemed too self-serving. What I did realize in my relief was that over the years, the worry about CO status and the effort for it became so single-minded that the quest turned into an end in itself. My mind-set was not as intense as the trance Skip would come to realize he was in, in which "you are on a production line: you go to an ambush site, fight, do a body count, return to camp, and do this again and again. You lose yourself in the fluidity of the moment." But the faith that drove me to declare myself a conscientious objector was often overshadowed by the fluidity of my concentrated determination to be acknowledged as one and not have to face prison rather than fight in a war.

Home for Christmas, 1969, age twenty-five

My life was my own again. Some poor guy would take my place— and considering how the rules favored the educated and the wealthy, even with the lottery, he likely would be some poor, poor guy. My choice and conviction put someone else in harm's way.

Skip's life still belonged to Uncle Sam. In his first nine months in Vietnam, he and his men blew more than thirty ambushes. All were harrowing, but perhaps the most harrowing of all was the one in a former Michelin rubber plantation, an area they often patrolled. Skip had received intelligence that there was a contingent of sixty to seventy-five Vietcong somewhere among the trees, and he and his twenty men moved silently through them, looking and listening for telltale signs or sounds. Skip knew he had entered their perimeter when he recognized a nearly imperceptible brushwork marking, left "so when the VC go to crap, they know where they're moving beyond their perimeter."

His point man made a signal to stop. "We could hear them making dinner, and I knew if we made noise they would be onto us. We couldn't disengage from them, so the only thing I could do is make them move toward me," which would allow his men the first shot, because movement betrays position.

The way to do that was to make it seem that he and his men were behind the others, and that required artillery stationed many miles away to fire shells that would drop to the rear of the Vietcong position. American soldiers had astonishing firepower at their disposal, which could turn someone like Skip into Zeus, capable of hurling deadly fire bolts—although he was very much in their path, as well. As only fifteen yards at one point separated the two groups of soldiers, Skip, and those firing, had to be very precise. He checked the coordinates he had jotted down in his New Testament.

He signaled groups of men to make cloverleaf patrols (a few men peel off the line of advance and circle back to the left or right), which would help guide him and allow him to better detect where the enemy was. Then, in a series of radio commands, "I brought artillery in from the rear and walked it in closer and closer, to make them think we were coming in behind them." He then ordered a change of direction, so the shells were literally coming over him and Pat Hewitt, one of his squad leaders, as they lay pressed to the ground. "You could feel the whiz of the shell. We were lucky they didn't hit us. I was good at doing artillery, but as Pat said to me, 'This is *awful* chancy.' I remember turning to him and saying, 'Patrick, I know what I'm doing,' but I was making it up and expecting big casualties."

Just as planned, the shelling sent the Vietcong streaming toward Skip's platoon "When these guys started to run over us, we fired. We brought in the world on these characters. It was pretty awful." Afterward, the rubber plantation was in disarray, "but you could still see the corridors between the trees. We just walked down them." Skip later was awarded the Silver Star for his leadership. Outnumbered three to one, all of his men were alive in the end. All the Vietcong were dead

In the ambushes Skip blew, not a single soldier under his command was killed, and only two were truly seriously injured: a machine gunner with a sucking chest wound and a sergeant who lost an arm. Skip was never wounded by enemy fire, though he still has grenade fragments in his back—from his own grenade. "We had movement and I was throwing grenades—you use a grenade as an area weapon because after the explosion they can't see where it came from—and I didn't duck low enough. As Dave Rogers said to me—he always had something reasonable and sardonic to say—while he took out the fragments one by one and dropped them into his inverted metal helmet, 'You—*clank!*—are—*clank!*—one—*clank!*—fucking—*clank!*—stupid—*clank!*— son—*clank!*—of—*clank!*—a—*clank!*—bitch.' "

Skip's ability to protect his men while amassing a high enemy body count caught the attention of Gen. Herbert E. Wolf, the assistant division commander of the First Infantry Division. "He liked that I was getting a high body count with no casualties."

Wolf, a distinguished soldier, was born in Germany in 1925 to a family that fled the Nazis and relocated in the United States. He tried to enlist in the army when he turned eighteen but was rejected as an "enemy alien." Shortly thereafter, in the army's infinite wisdom, he was drafted and served as a private first class in the Philippines. In 1945, he was awarded a battlefield commission for his role in a raid on a Japanese prisoner-of-war camp that rescued 511 American soldiers, and after Vietnam, he went on to command what is today the U.S. Army, Pacific.

At Wolf's suggestion, a team from the Pentagon came out to watch Lieutenant Packard and his men in action to figure out what he was doing that made him so successful. What they saw made Wolf want Skip's tactics to be the norm, and for his last months in Vietnam, Skip was again a teacher, this time instructing new officers.

As he counted down his days remaining in-country, he thought about his future. Returning to law school had no appeal; he realized he had "sort of sold myself" previously that the law was what he wanted to do. In what he calls "the trance" of Vietnam, he felt the tug of the church. A fellow officer with priestly ambitions shared with Skip his books by Pierre Teilhard de Chardin, the French Jesuit, paleontologist, and philosopher who died in 1955. His teaching is that Christian theology combined with human evolution is leading mankind to a higher level, one of peace and unity with themselves and the Earth.

That sense of unity and reconciliation was a wholly different one from what was required of a soldier in Vietnam, and its hope helped lead Skip to apply to Virginia Theological Seminary in Alexandria, the second-oldest and the largest of the Episcopal seminaries, which accepted him.

The movie on the chartered flight that took Skip and a couple of hundred other soldiers home from Vietnam in March 1970 was Francis Ford Coppola's 1968 adaptation of *Finian's Rainbow*, with Fred Astaire, Petula Clark, and Tommy Steele. He cried as he watched it, overcome by the "sense of relief that I had made it, that I didn't die, that it was over and I was going home to see people I loved. And also because I left a lot of bodies behind, all unnamed."

M y years of nightmares of being in prison were based on anxiety about what might happen. They stopped when prison was no longer a threat and have been replaced by those that come from the general anxieties of life. Skip's nightmares, however, began after he left Vietnam. They hideously replay what he had to do to stay alive, and they have held him prisoner for decades.

Seven

There might be a more polar opposite to leading ambush and patrol in Vietnam than seminary, but it was enough of one for Skip. The life lessons, and the taking-of-life lessons, that made him such a success in the Hobbesian jungle were useless in the gentlemanly confines of Virginia Theological Seminary, which he entered in September 1970.

"When you're in Vietnam," he said many years after his return, when he had gained perspective, "on the platoon level, you can do anything you want; you're king of the world. What do you do with that kind of level of success? And then Vietnam's over"—he clapped his hands—"what do you do with it? Where do you go with it? I could have stayed in the army, but that wasn't a good idea. You can only do what I did in the army over there. At home is a whole different story." He did, however, stay in the U.S. Army Reserves.

And he had a name change. At Fort Benning and in Vietnam, he was known not as "Skip," but as "Packard," or "Lieutenant," or, by his platoon, as simply "3–6." To his new colleagues, he was "George," and has been known as that since. He continued to sign his letters to me "Skip," but as the years have progressed, now only his siblings and I and those who knew him in college use the nickname.

At first, seminary was not what he expected. He quickly learned that it "wanted no part of the story of Vietnam," which to me mocked the idea of a Christian institution devoted to the training of priests who can understand guilt and shame, for surely those are parts of human nature and were two of Skip's strongest feelings. It seems as if many of his fellow seminarians were, for whatever reason, there to escape exposure to what Skip had seen and done. He was chronologically a few years older than most of his classmates but a lifetime ahead in understanding the sins of the world and the horrors that mankind can commit, two useful pieces of knowledge for a priest. Skip was at once remorseful over what he had done in Vietnam and defensive in the face of the indifference that greeted him, not only at the seminary but from many Americans who could not separate the war from the warriors. And then there was his own self-reproach. The "crazy, insane things" he had done "were not just. I had to deal with the consequences. I'd always wondered about the moral consequences of killing people. I've killed people. And they *say* you feel okay because it was in defense of this country. But how can you say this war was in defense of this country?"

For someone who had always been elected to positions

of leadership in school and until recently had been king of the world with his platoon, seminary quickly proved that there was a new world order. The easily elected president of the student body at Hobart now felt "self-conscious and out of place," suddenly aware that "I couldn't rely on the impact of a former social skill." For the first time, his expectations were out of sync with reality.

Plus, he now had to cope with the shadow world of post-traumatic stress disorder, which haunted his dreams and distorted reality, and which, in those days, "you couldn't share with anybody and it just kind of played out." Skip was a wreck. There were intense exchanges with his wife, and flashbacks during which he was convinced he was still in the jungle, hunting and being hunted.

When Skip was in the third or fourth grade, he had a recurring nightmare in which he was engulfed by a deafening silence. That silence scared him terribly. But in a few months, the nightmares stopped, and he did not feel that silence again until he was in seminary. At first, "It really freaked me out. There's this breathy moment of waiting as you hear the silence. Then all of a sudden I said, I know this silence. I know it! It was the same silence that would wake me up in fourth grade, and I just put it away from myself." But it could be, he came to realize, "a contemplative sound that is a very sweet place to be," and it helped him as he came to believe that God could be found within it.

"It started to do strange things to me. In seminary I learned about silence and the Quaker way, and I said, I'm not crazy; this is where I'm supposed to be."

In June 1974, he earned a Master of Divinity degree

and was ordained a deacon; that December, he was ordained a priest, and he transferred from the infantry to become a chaplain in the U.S. Army Reserve.

Skip's enrollment in seminary coincided with my changing secular vocations. After holding a number of interesting and varied positions in the Peace Corps, I now spent more than half the year flying around the world to evaluate in-country and training programs. It was a great job, with one exception: I was twenty-six years old and I was telling people twice my age what they were doing wrong. It was time to make my own mistakes. I took up writing, a profession in which there is never a shortage of critics.

Around the time Skip entered seminary, my father made a big change in his life as well, having decided to retire. In eighteen years, he had taken St. Alban's from a tiny mission with a few score members to a thriving parish with a congregation of more than six hundred. This advancement was largely due to his leadership and personality, but it came at a personally taxing price of two large building-fund campaigns that had met their goals and then some. The latest had been to build a day school for kindergarten through fourth grade. Additions were needed, but my father was about to turn sixty-five and felt he didn't have the stamina to lead another fund drive. He and my mother had long dreamed of traveling the world by freighter and camper and agreed now was the time.

Over a period of several years, my parents drove their camper across Europe and used my two spinster aunts' home in Elsecar as a base. They managed this on their small Social Security benefits and my father's smaller pension, and they seemed to love every minute. I went to visit them during one of their stopovers in Elsecar. One night, my father and I were leaning on the bar of the George and Dragon, the pub my mother's grandmother's family had owned in nearby Wentworth, and our talk turned to the surprising number of times he was asked to assist or take services as they traveled, and to the institutional Church.

"The Church is filled with people who should never be priests," he said, more in wonder than in anger, "They have their heads buried completely away from the world. They don't know how to deal with sex or drugs or any of the other real things that are part of life. They spout platitudes and hide behind dogma. When I started hearing sermon after sermon, week after week, in church after church, I was astounded by how often it was given by someone who is simply incompetent. I can only hope I wasn't that foolish or scared. As for the Church, it is more big business than it is Christianity."

He did not have to worry about appearing foolish. As I've mentioned, my father was not a dramatic speaker, and his sermons rarely lasted more than ten minutes, but he was very effective in that short time. He preached as if he were just talking with the congregation, as he did with me at the bar that night. His messages were instructive of faith, and they clearly and often profoundly stated the core of Christianity. An example is one of his last Easter sermons:

Everyone wonders why churches should be so crowded on Easter Sunday, and why people who never go to church should get up early and attend sunrise services. It seems to be one of the mysteries of life, that people who never darken the doors of a church should make such a point of going at Easter.

They believe that Christ is risen but have never understood that He is alive.

There is a world of difference between these two statements. So many people can grasp the Creed up to Easter. They believe Christ lived a perfect life, that He was crucified on Good Friday, and that somehow He came into His own on Easter Day. And that is the end of the story for them. Christ is risen but He has "gone."

Easter is a commemoration of a historical event, not a celebration of a glorious, present reality. I can remember a church in England, with the words over the altar, "He is not here; He is risen," and that is the thinking of so many people.

The glorious fact which the Apostles found was that Christ was not only risen but alive. The empty tomb might be a symbol of Christ's victory, but of itself it would be a tame ending to the story.

The Easter hope is based more on Christ's appearance to His disciples.

The Easter gospel is that Christ is *alive,* and that the Holy Spirit is even now at work in the world, making Him known to us.

It was this that gave the early Christians their energy—inspired the first teachings of the Gospel— the first martyrdoms, and the first saints.

It was not an absent Christ but a *present* Christ who presided over the Church.

You can picture the horror of parents whose child is missing—the anxious waiting, the heartbreaking suspense—and the joy when the child is found alive. That was the joy of the disciples.

The introit [what he read at the opening of the service] for today is from St. Paul's Letter to the Romans. Here it is again:

"Now if we have died with Christ, we believe that we will also live with Him. We know that Christ, being raised from the dead, will never die again; death no longer has dominion over Him. For the death He died He died to sin, once and for all, but the life He lives He lives to God. So you also must consider yourselves dead to sin and alive to God in Christ Jesus."

"Dead to sin" and "Alive to God" have more than a moral meaning. They do not simply mean that you stop leading bad lives and start leading good ones, not does it mean that your life, previously centered around the home and the golf course, is now centered around the Church.

There are two areas where this makes a difference: In worship, instead of hymns, prayers, lessons, and sacraments commemorating past events, we realize they are celebrating present realities. And instead of coming to church to hear about Christ, we have come to meet Him. We come to church not from a duty, but with expectancy and faith to meet a *living* God.

Our daily conduct is transformed. If Christ were just risen, all we could do would be to try to fulfill the teachings of a lost leader. But because He is still alive, we walk under the directions of a *living* leader.

Christianity is not obedience to a moral code, but a relationship with a living Lord.

Consequently, we ourselves become free and alive.

Our Lord is not there, but *here,* and we are walking in the life of immortality *right now.*

While all through his ministry my father felt that he walked under the direction of a living leader and for a very long time I did as well, shortly after I turned thirty I noticed a drift away from my secure faith. It was a course of omission, not commission—of what I happened not to do rather than what I decided to do. I no longer attended services every Sunday and found I didn't really miss them, so I went even less often, though I never missed Christmas, Ash Wednesday, or Easter. Fewer and fewer in my circle of friends were devout, and Sunday mornings increasingly were devoted to sleeping in, followed by a leisurely read of the paper. I still felt connected to the Episcopal Church and closely followed its internal doings through clergy friends and my parents, but it was more an institutional attachment I felt than one that connected me with God. I derived a sense of inclusion and security from my relationships with the bishops and clergy I knew well and liked, and who liked me. I felt part of the Church, an insider in a genteel and socially prominent faith. Unfortunately, this meant that I found comfort more in feeling connected to the establishment than to the Holy Spirit.

What is surprising now is that this didn't start sooner. My faith until then had been completely by the book (of Common Prayer). I totally accepted what the Church taught, and to that degree was a good Christian. In sentiment, I was like Parson Thwackum in *Tom Jones,* who tells the philosopher Mr. Square, "When I say religion, I mean the Christian religion; and when I say the Christian religion, I mean the Protestant religion; and when I say the Protestant religion, I mean the Church of England." The parson is a perfect hypocrite: He spouts Christian teaching while looking out only for himself. I like to think my shared value of the Church was more spiritually based. But as we are taught that we have free will, it seems a bit odd that I never questioned what was instilled in me until well into my adulthood.

Two reasons I didn't and held so closely to what I had always believed were my parents, my father especially. I attached so much of my belief to his actions and leadership that I had no interest in believing other than he did. It had worked well for him, it had worked well all this time for me, and, hewing closely to the Fifth Commandment— Honor thy father and thy mother—I saw no reason to challenge or change what I believed. Of course that was not the whole of it. I thought that to break with the established faith of home would be to break with my parents and to disappoint them in a way I was unprepared to do. I had always been a good and dutiful son, and even when I was in my thirties, I liked it that when someone said complimentary things about me to my father, his reply was still, "He's a block off the old chip." I disengaged from my parents as a daily force in my life in the usual separation that comes with independence, but in matters of faith, apart from declaring myself a CO, I was not yet my own person. Once I was clear of the draft, there was not an imperative to concentate on my convictions. It's not that I had never doubted my beliefs, just that the doubts never went deep or lasted for long, and to the extent they did exist, I hid them from my parents and acted as if nothing were amiss, and thus became something of a Thwackum myself.

In February 1976, after being bothered for a couple of months by a dry, ticklish cough that wouldn't go away, my father went to see his doctor. An X-ray showed a spot on his right lung about the size of a quarter. My father called to tell me the news. The doctor felt the tumor was isolated and contained and could be easily cut out. He wanted to operate right away, but my father postponed the surgery for a week so he could marry a longtime friend of mine and her fiancé on Valentine's Day. He would have the surgery the morning after. "Don't worry," he told me, and don't bother to come to California. "Everything is going to be fine." I put on a good show of accepting this, but I was worried and scared.

On the day of his surgery, he looked like this: five-six, with thinning black-and-gray hair. A tanned bald spot atop his head topped a tanned body with a generous, though not excessive, girth; until he was about fifty, he was very thin. He wore trifocals to focus nearly black eyes. He had a weathered face (he played golf every week) and laugh lines.

I waited by the phone for my mother's call after the surgery. When it came, my fear was justified. The doctor had found the small tumor right where it was supposed to be. It *was* the size of a quarter, and slow-growing to boot, and if that had been all there was, he would have been fine in six weeks. But the X-ray had *not* shown a mass of rapidly growing cancer that covered the base of both lungs, hugged the vena cava like a hungry lover, and was impossible to resect. The surgeon surveyed the mess and sewed my father up without even touching the lungs with his scalpel.

As my father had smoked a pack of cigarettes a day for thirty-five years, this was not completely surprising, but it was somewhat ironic. He had given up smoking twelve years earlier, when the surgeon general's report on the now-proven dangers of smoking was published and convinced him that smoking wasn't good for his health.

Until the discovery of his cancer, the sickest he had ever been was with an occasional three-day virus that laid him low—laid him out on the couch, actually, where he wrapped himself in an afghan and had me bring him a hot buttered rum. "For the cough," he would say. "Soothes the throat."

He was seventy-one years old but looked sixty before the operation. After it, he looked and felt ninety. But then he had a couple of months of great remission, and when he turned seventy-two in June, things were looking up. He played golf. He did push-ups. His humor remained intact. He came home one day from the store with a calculator he had bought for $11.98. "Look at this," he said as he turned it on. "It adds. Subtracts. Multiplies. Divides. Does percentages. Why, it has all the advantages of the twelve-dollar model!"

He had been given a heavy dose of radiation on the off chance it would help, and to the doctors' surprise, it was working wonderfully. He felt good. His appetite came back from the total apathy he had had toward food for the first six weeks following surgery. The doctor who had told me after the operation that 95 percent of the people with lung cancer like my father's died within the year subsequently said that on paper my father was dead, but that proved how much paper knew. Still later he showed me X-rays of how the tumor had shrunk. "A couple more months like this and we may be back in business," he said. "If anyone has connections with God, your father has, and it looks like they're paying off."

Any connections that improved my father's health were severed the day his voice went in early August. He could barely whisper when I talked with him on the phone. While he and my mother were saying it was only a slight case of laryngitis, it didn't seem so to me. A recent girlfriend of mine at that time was an oncologist and she used to discuss her cases with me. From what I had learned, it sounded as if the tumor had started up again. When, three days later, he woke up from a nap with terrible back pains, I was certain the stampede of malignancy had begun.

It happened that I was going to visit my parents in a couple of days anyway. Though we talked and corresponded often in the ten years since my graduation from college, I saw my parents only two or three times a year. By the time they resettled in El Cajon in a double-wide trailer after their world travels, I was settled in Manhattan. My father's stipend from the church pension fund was a whopping $350 a month, and because he had always lived in a rectory, they had no equity in a home. This was the best they could do, and they happily swapped the little monetary reward the Church offered for the greater reward they received through ministry.

I went to see them not in the double-wide but in a beachfront house loaned to them by vacationing friends. The morning after I arrived, my father had an early appointment with the doctor to have new tests and X-rays, and I was scheduled to play chauffeur for the twenty-mile drive to the hospital. We'd know the results the next day.

That afternoon, I sat in the sun, making a show of doing work in honor of the unspoken agreement we had not to sit around wringing our hands. My father came out and pulled up a chair beside me.

"Let's face it," he said with little delay. "I'm not long for this world. I'm not afraid to die and I don't think it will happen for a while. But this will probably kill me, and it's not much of a life having no energy and being in pain anyway. So I want to ask you to look out for your mother. That doesn't mean take full responsibility for her or move out here. Just look out for her, okay?" So this is what it's like, I thought. Your father comes out into the sunshine and asks that you look out for your mother after he dies. And as much: Look out for yourself.

When the phone rang the next afternoon, my mother

was outside and my father and I were reading in the living room. "You answer it," he said in his strained whisper; "my voice isn't strong enough."

It was the doctor. There were no surprises. The cancer had gone to his bones. My father would be given chemotherapy, but the outlook was bleak. "We can do a lot to reduce the pain," the doctor told me, "but he has four, maybe five months at best. Bring him in tomorrow and I'll show him the scans and the X-rays and explain what we can do next."

It fell to me to tell my father that he would soon die.

"It was the doctor," I said. "The cancer is in your bones. The tumor is spreading." In my head I was yelling at myself to keep my voice steady and my eyes dry as I repeated what the doctor had told me. I half-succeeded: My voice was half-steady; my eyes were half-dry. The last thing either of us needed was for me not to finish. "I love you very much," I said with some evenness. "I don't think I could have had a better father." He nodded and looked calm. "Thank you, son," he said, and we looked at each other for several seconds. Then he said, "Come on, split a beer with me."

We had a couple more that afternoon, too. When my mother came in, my father told her the news. No one said much else. We all moved out into the sun. My mother took a snapshot. It is of my father, on a chaise longue, with the Pacific at his left hand, a glass of beer raised in his right, and a broad grin on his face.

I left California two or three days later, and a few days after that, there was a letter from my father: "I took chemo-therapy last Monday with seemingly good results, so far. Great stuff, chemo-therapy. Your urine turns orange color, you are nauseated and vomit, and your hair falls out, but it's great stuff—all the doctors say so. Be that as it may, I am feeling much better, and do odd things around the house, like sleeping."

With my father's condition seemingly stabilized, I didn't expect to go back to California for a month, but in two weeks, the phone rang. It was seven o'clock on a Monday evening for me, four in the afternoon for them. My father was in the hospital. He had collapsed while seeing the doctor. It would be a matter of hours, days at most, before his heart could no longer pump blood through his embolismic lungs. I talked with the doctor. I talked with my mother. I talked with my father.

"Well, this is it," he said in that near voice.

"Just don't do anything rash until I get there."

"It'll be nice to see you. Here's Mother."

I caught the first plane to San Diego and was by my father's bedside by lunchtime. He looked awful. An oxygen tube was in his nose, an intravenous tube in his right arm. His color was gray, which matched the food on his plate. Beside the bed was not a Bible or the Book of Common Prayer, as might be expected, but instead a copy of *Alice in Wonderland*.

"Hi, son," he said. "Here, have some of this food. I can't eat it all."

Who could? The sugar package had a picture of the Torrey Pines golf course on one side. On the other side it said, "Enjoy yourself! You're dining in the playground of Southern California."

There is not much to talk about with someone who is

concentrating on staying alive, but we had plenty to distract us. My father was no stranger to this hospital. For more than twenty-five years, he had been coming here to see parishioners and to give last rites and to comfort families. So doctors and nurses who knew him popped in, and a lab technician who noticed his name on a vial came up, and various clergy friends came and went after leaving a prayer floating over the bed. As for me, I wandered in and out. My father didn't want me just sitting around on a deathwatch, and neither did I. So I went for walks, called friends in New York in the hope of easing my pain and fear, sat by him for a spell. After he toyed with his dinner, my mother and I went to a nearby restaurant. She had spent the night sitting by his bed, but, because she had been a registered nurse and through her faith was certain of my father's next destination, she was calm and ready for whatever was to happen. One thing that was going to happen, my father told her, was that she was going home that night with me. Over dinner, I asked her to visit me in New York as soon as she was ready, and she said she would. This went so smoothly that it was like slow motion.

We returned to the hospital after dinner, and before we left, my mother took a walk while my father and I talked, and in what seemed a natural flow of conversation, he gave his last homily, a variation on the theme of several of his letters and our talks over the years.

"If you take the Bible and look closely, you'll see Christianity comes down to only one thing," he said softly. "That is to love one another. The miracles are all window dressing."

It would be dramatic but untrue to say that my mother

and I slept that night with an ear open for the phone; we slept like stones. When we got to the hospital, my father was in decent spirits after an uncomfortable night. He needed a shave but, with his tubes and general weakness, couldn't handle it himself. So I took an electric razor and did it for him, remembering that on Saturday mornings when I was about seven my father and I would go into the bathroom, where he would whirl his shaving brush around the soap bowl and lather his face and I would take an old brush and do the same. Then we would shave—he with a new blade, I with an empty razor.

The next morning, an attendant came into the room to check the oxygen flow to my father. "This is too high," he announced, and turned it way down. I asked him to turn it back up and check his information; I had been there when the doctor said it should be so high. Another attendant came in, followed by a nurse. They debated whether the flow should be up or down. My father complained that water was condensing in his nose from the oxygen, so one of the attendants took the nosepiece off to change it. The debate over pressure continued while the nosepiece stayed out. My father began to look like a fish out of water. "Get the oxygen back to him immediately," I yelled. The tube was replaced, but the pressure was not elevated; one attendant stayed behind to be sure I didn't touch the regulator while the other went to check. My father's discomfort continued. The first attendant finally returned and set the flow as high as it had been; then he and the second attendant and the nurse left without a word. CO be damned: I wanted to suffocate them all.

A few hours later, I drove home to get the mail for my

mother and run a couple of errands. In this time long before cell phones, I called the hospital from home before going back, to see if I should bring anything. "Just yourself," my mother said. "Your father's having trouble."

I drove the seven miles to the hospital in fewer minutes, rehearsing all the way what I would say to the Highway Patrolman who might stop me doing ninety on the uncrowded freeway, but it turned out to be a speech I could save. The figures in my father's room were a deathbed tableau. Two nurses bent over him, one with a blood-pressure collar, another holding his arm. My mother held his hand. "Let me go," he was saying, clearly to the nurses, "let me go."

"Hi, Dad," I said.

He opened his eyes. "Oh, hello, son." The nurses backed off as I went to the other side of the bed. My father rolled over to greet me. I caught him in my arms. Within a minute, his body had rattled itself quiet.

The nurses left, and one called for an attendant to take away the body. My mother and I sat at the end of the bed. There wasn't much to say as we tried to collect ourselves and contemplated the future without him, but when after thirty minutes no one had come, we started to get fidgety. My father was covered from head to foot with a bedsheet, and his toes jutted up. I stood and grabbed a foot and shook it lightly, and his body moved a bit as well. "Why didn't you take it with you?" I asked. My mother giggled, and so did I. For all our grief, we both were relieved that my father was no longer suffering. He could have hung around in misery for months. He had seen a lot of lingering death in his visits to sick parishioners, and I think he knew better. It's one thing to have a lucky life, the doctor told me later; it's another to have a lucky death. I thought that a strange juxtaposition at the time but soon learned it isn't. My father was lucky both ways.

L ater that week, there was a memorial service at St. Alban's. It was a hot, still, relentlessly sunny day, and as there was no air-conditioning, the temperature in the church was over one hundred degrees, the air made hotter by the overflow of mourners who packed the pews. Almost all the local clergy were there as well, close to forty of them, in black cassocks and white surpluses and black stoles. As they made their way up the aisle at the start of the service, heartily singing "For All the Saints (Who from Their Labors Rest)," I had a vision of an elephant burial ground and all the beasts trumpeting over their fallen compatriot. I nearly laughed and was grateful for the momentary respite from my sorrow. There was no casket; my father had already been cremated.

After the service, we all gathered in the parish hall, everyone drenched with sweat, for lemonade and punch, sandwiches and cookies. My mother and I greeted everyone and reminisced and said our thanks for their kind words and obvious affection for my father. After the last had gone, we walked out and I saw the railing I had bent over as I threw up on those Sunday mornings twenty-five years before and it all came back to me: the counting of the communicants, the tallying of the offering, the bacon and eggs and scurrying to be back in church for the 9:15

service. That world, already long past, was now officially gone.

It took no time to decide what to do with my father's ashes. My father loved being at Camp Stevens, loved celebrating Communion in the open air of the chapel, and was grateful that he had the chance to help make this special place apart from everyday life a piece of the lives of so many people over so many years. On a beautifully clear autumn day six weeks after my father's death, my mother and I and a dozen friends and Boone Sadler—his good friend and the priest who had found the camp property with him twenty years earlier—and Boone's wife met there to disperse the ashes. My mother had made a few sandwiches, which she packed in a picnic hamper, and I'd picked up a couple of bottles of wine to have with lunch afterward. We parked near where we were going to scatter the ashes and everyone but Boone and I walked ahead. He opened the trunk and I retrieved the small cardboard box that held my father's remains.

We went down the dirt road by the swimming pool where I had roamed the deck as lifeguard. Beside the pool were trees I had planted in the summer of 1963, which were now thirty feet tall. It had taken me a day to dig through the hardpan to plant them, and I remember muttering the whole time that the then camp director was crazy for wanting them there, because the prevailing wind would blow the leaves into the pool. I was right, but the camp director was an ex–marine sergeant major who didn't like backtalk. "See?" I said to no one as we passed the leaf-strewn pool.

Camp Stevens chapel, ca. 1980

At the end of the one-hundred-yard-long path is the open-air chapel, where the others had already gathered. They had been joined by some local folks who knew my father, as well as by the camp staff, and Happy, the dog that belonged to the current camp director and his wife. They were all standing in the clearing, surrounded by pine and black oak trees and manzanita bushes.

"Unto Almighty God we commend the soul of our brother departed," Boone recited from the Book of Common Prayer, "and we commit his body to the ground; earth to earth, ashes to ashes, dust to dust; in sure and certain hope of the Resurrection unto eternal life. . . ."

At the end of the prayer, Boone and I took the box with its mixture of ashes and granulated bone a few yards behind the altar, where a valley begins and where leaves and rain and snow would quickly take all trace of them away, and we dug into the box like farmers into a bag of seed, each getting a handful, and tossed the gray residue out as if we were sowing a field. Whereupon Happy leaped out after them. I laughed. My mother laughed. People who thought they shouldn't tried to stifle their laughs. They needn't have. My father would have told the story for years.

I often dreamed of my father in the months after he died and the ones I remember were variations of those many people in similar circumstances report, where I was on one side of a river and my father was on the opposite bank. But about six months after his death, I had a strikingly different dream. We met on the sidewalk between the church and the rectory; I was walking away from the church and he toward it. He was dressed in his black suit and clerical collar, so I assumed he was on assignment and didn't have time for a long visit. We greeted each other fondly; then I told him I knew he was in a hurry but that I had two quick questions.

"Ask away," he said.

"How am I doing?"

"You're doing okay. Could be better but could be worse," he said kindly. "What's your other question?"

"What can you tell me about God?" His answer came immediately.

"God is no Kleenex," he said, and walked on.

I've pondered—and laughed at—this answer ever since. I had, in fact, already begun my separation from the Church and so my walking away from the one in the dream made literal sense. As for the Kleenex, what can I say? God isn't to be sneezed at? Maybe because all my life my father had told me that God is love, he assumed I would have remembered what God *is* rather than what He is not. Perhaps the lesson to be learned here is that, believe in God or not, He can't, as I experience every day, be easily disposed of.

M y father's death loosened my tie to the Church and to my faith even more. The reason is pretty simple. He was in many ways the conduit to my spiritual life, and his death made me look for another connection, which I have yet to satisfactorily find; it turned out that for me, the Father in the Lord's Prayer was less in heaven than he was in El Cajon. But there is more to it than that. I loved the rites and rituals of the Episcopal Church without question or doubt for the first thirty years of my life. Then one day while reciting the Nicene Creed, I realized that accepting this lengthy statement of belief whole was like swallowing a camel, and I began to give thought to each part. From there, doubt about the words of many prayers crept in. The Nicene and Apostles' Creeds make so many specific assertions about the nature of God and Jesus Christ that faith is like a pinned butterfly. More and more I liked the idea of leading a good life without having to frame it with dogma about original sin, ascension into heaven, and who is sitting at God's right hand. This was not, however, something I felt I could discuss with my mother, a lovely, caring, compassionate woman who adored me but who, in matters of religion, was rigidly dogmatic.

A way to understand one's faith is to give it the Peter, Paul, and Mary test. Saint Peter believed in Jesus, but for every step he took forward, he often took two back. It was Peter who, in Saint Mark's Gospel, proclaimed true faith and then later, over a period of several hours, three times denied knowing Christ in the Garden of Gethsemane and before Pilate.

Saint Paul began, as he wrote of himself first in Philippians and then in Galatians, as Saul "of the stock of Israel, of the tribe of Benjamin, an Hebrew of the Hebrews," who "violently persecuted" the early Christians. Then came his dramatic conversion: Around A.D. 33, while walking on the road from Jerusalem to Damascus, he had a vision of the risen Jesus that left him temporarily blind and permanently as staunch a Christian as he had been an opponent. He became the unswerving articulator of faith through the letters he wrote to the congregations in Greece, Galatia (now Turkey), and Rome, which constitute much of the New Testament.

And Mary, the mother of Jesus, simply believed Him in everything.

My mother was a Mary: It's in the Bible; it's a fact. As the bumper sticker puts it, "Jesus said it, I believe it, that settles it."

Not long after my father died, on a visit home I brought Nobel Prize physicist Steven Weinberg's book *The First Three Minutes: A Modern View of the Origin of the Universe*. My mother took one look at the title and asked, "Does it mention God's role?" Nor was she someone to engage in theological uncertainty. Shortly after my wife, Karen—a descendant of the founder of Reformed Judaism on one side, raised an Episcopalian by her mother on the other, graduate of a Quaker prep school—and I were married, my mother asked her if she believed Jesus Christ was the son of God.

"I believe that Jesus believed He was the son of God," Karen replied, trying hard neither to offend nor be insincere.

"So," my mother shot back, "you're saying He's a liar?"

I didn't speak with my mother about my changing faith. I just went to church with her.

My reading of saints and philosophers bolstered my faith for decades. In decline, I found help elsewhere. In many ways, the writer most responsible for helping me articulate my ebbing faith is Woody Allen. The two of us have regularly talked about his work and ideas since 1971, and at first, I thought he had staked out a position rich for use in comedy but one that was impoverished spiritually. A few years after my father's death, however, I found myself more open to his rationalist, humanistic view. Woody's conviction (and annoyance) is that as much as we might like there to be a personal God in a universe where wrongdoing is punished and virtue rewarded, we only kid ourselves into comfort by believing it. His aphorisms and observations about God, religion, and faith are widely quoted, in part because they're pithy and funny and in part because they lead to reflection. A few:

"If it turns out there is a God, I don't think that He's evil. I think the worst you can say about Him is that basically He's an underachiever" [*Love and Death,* 1975].

"To you, I'm an atheist; to God, I'm the loyal opposition" [*Stardust Memories,* 1980].

"Faith is the path of least resistance" [*Match Point,* 2005].

"I wish it were so," Skip said after he read this last quote. "It's hard to throw your lot into being intentionally faithful, because faith is a very elusive thing. It would be great if God was in a chair, carrying on a conversation—though sometimes I do have that sense—but often there is just a long silence; as if there's no one home and then—if you're alert for it—bingo! A subtlety happens and a silence has the appearance of being self-imposed."

A number of Woody's films examine the question of crime and punishment in a godless universe, or at least a universe with an uncaring God. *Match Point* is the story of a man who commits a murder and, though at first considered a suspect, is cleared when someone killed in a drug deal gone bad is circumstantially tied to the murder. As with the killer in *Crimes and Misdemeanors* (1989), he has no qualms of conscience and so lives on unaffected. *Cassandra's Dream* (2007) takes the opposite, Dostoyevskian tack: A murderer who is never considered a suspect is undone by his conscience.

These films are often treated seriously in theological circles. In one of our conversations after *Match Point* came out, Woody said:

"A Catholic priest wrote about the movie. It was very nice, but he made a wrong assumption. The assumption was: If, as I say, life is meaningless and chaos and random, then anything goes and nothing has any meaning and one action is as good as the next. And it immediately leads someone with a religious agenda to the conclusion, Well, you can just murder people and get away with it if that's what you want to do. But that's a false conclusion. What I'm really saying—and it's not hidden or esoteric—is that we have to accept that the universe is godless and life is meaningless, often a terrible and brutal experience with no hope, and that love relationships are very, very hard, and that we still need to find a way to not only cope but lead a decent and moral life. . . .

"You're in a lifeboat with other people and you've got to try and make it as decent as you can for yourself and everybody. And it would seem to me this is so much more moral and even much more 'Christian.'"

My father died just at the time that Woody moved from out-and-out comedies to films that, among other topics, considered God's presence or absence, so while my father laughed at *Take the Money and Run* and *Bananas* and appreciated Woody as a comedian, we never had a chance to talk about his more serious ideas. I wish we had. In *Crimes and Misdemeanors,* there is a line written by Woody that my father would have agreed with: "It is only we, with our capacity to love, that give meaning to the indifferent universe." Though, of course, my father would have added that our capacity to love comes from God and is a reflection of Him.

One day, I talked about Woody with a deeply Christian friend possessed of a certainty of God's love and availability. "It must be very lonely for him," my friend said, thinking of life without a caring Creator who can be reached through prayer and meditation. Well, yes, he and the existentialists (with the exception of Søren Kierkegaard, the father of existentialism but also a devout Christian) would agree with that. Faith puts us in the warm and embracing company of fellow believers and Almighty God. I can attest that it is a wonderful place to be, if you can believe it to be true. (Although as Skip and David Rogers and Chester Davis experienced, the warm embracing company of fellow believers is sometimes in violent surroundings, in which they risk their lives on behalf of others.)

A few months after my dad died, Skip phoned to say that it was time for me to honor my father's calling. After seminary, Skip had become the assistant at a small parish in Virginia and then quickly was called to be the rector of a large, prosperous parish in the southern part of the state, and he wanted me to talk to his congregation about my time in the Peace Corps and then give a short homily at a service. I had mixed feelings about this. My father had been the priest. I was someone trying to makes sense of a God who heretofore had been plain to me, but Skip was my buddy and I wanted to see him. It was winter and my plane from New York was delayed by a snowstorm. Meanwhile, Skip had 150 congregants sitting in the parish hall, waiting for me to regale them. Since everyone was there, it was decided I would give my homily in person the next day, and after he hooked up a speakerphone at his end, I talked with him about our college days and my Peace Corps time from an open phone kiosk, much to the bafflement of my would-be copassengers, who couldn't help but hear me. I was able to get to Virginia the next morning and found that many of those who had listened the night before were waiting in the church for me to say something useful about faith. Then there would be questions and answers.

I had given what I was going to say many hours of thought and had written pages of junk, which I threw away before I left New York. In church, I stood up and looked out on so many expectant faces and, in no more than a minute, repeated what my father had told me as we leaned on the bar at the George and Dragon: "Love one another," I said. "That's what the Gospels come down to."

"Then you sat down," Skip recalled with a laugh as we talked about this in 2009. "Which is what you should do when the Spirit has spoken. But I thought, Well, we'll have to work something out of the Q and A session!" Which we did, and through Skip's mediation, what might have been a disaster turned out to be a lot of fun.

However, Skip's tenure at the Virginia parish was not entirely successful. There were complexities and undercurrents in the parish that, he says, his brief service as an assistant did not adequately prepare him for. "It was," he came to realize, "much too complicated for me. I was not centered enough or mature enough. I would say my whole relational life on any level was not what it should have been. I don't think my prayer life was that great, either. You can always tell: If something is happening with a priest and his or her prayers are a little wobbly, then other things tend to be a little shaky, too. The stabilizing factor is a sense that God is with you wherever you are, and you're at peace with where you are because God wants you there. You check in with Him and most of the times He's there, but sometimes He's not.

"In Vietnam you were very clear about what you needed to do. The enemy was there; you were here. In the case of a congregation, you spend a lot of your time in ad hoc groups from Sunday afternoon through the next Saturday, it's a sort of open calendar, and you have to be clear on how you function in this airy kind of environment. You can waste a lot of time. There are many priests who can do what they do in a week in a day and a half. A priest once said to me, 'The thing to do is go into church and praise God for what you're thankful for and then you realize there are things you are not thankful for.' But if you have expectations of doing things at a certain time of the day, you may be in for an education. I don't think I was successful doing this at first."

He accepted a part-time position at a parish in Hastings-on-Hudson, New York, thirty minutes north of New York City, where, he says, he was left to wonder, How did I get here? He experienced "a kind of a disconnection between social conversation and what was going on." He would awaken in the night, certain that he had killed someone when he was fifteen "and no one knew about it. I made it a secret and I brushed leaves over the body as I did in Vietnam. I was absolutely convinced that I had done this." It took a year or more of deep psychotherapy to really diagnose and begin to treat his post-traumatic stress disorder. Part of the trouble, he explains, was that his illness was "a bad blend—and tango—with obsessive-compulsive disorder. The clinical team treating me concluded that my OCD 'was a waiting receptacle for this psychosis.'

"You cannot understand how guys with PTSD are certain that the reality of what they are experiencing is reality. It's not," he told me years later; now he often helps people with the disorder. "It's a synthetic reality, but they don't know that. It's just unbelievable, unbelievable. I was so freaked out." And although he has the disorder in check, there are still vestiges of ambush and patrol that are ingrained in his senses. Perhaps it is why he and his men all escaped with their lives.

"I can't let someone sit behind me, like in a car," he told me one day over lunch as we sat at a corner table, he with his back to the wall. It was the day he recounted the firefight in the rubber plantation, using tableware as markers and taxicabs outside the window to show how close the combat was. The memory clearly upset him, but he was determined to tell me. I had ordered lightly and he was worried that I didn't have enough, so he kept offering me some of his meal. "I have difficulty when someone is sitting behind me in a train," he continued. "I have trouble sleeping." I suggested that something like he went through must permanently sharpen the senses. "Yes," he said. "It's hard to come down off that." He paused. "I watch hunting shows. There's something enjoyable about stalking. I can still feel the weight and ready balance of an M-16, the shallow breath, and clicking off the safety with the same finger that touches the trigger. It's a very conflicted feeling, devastating and terrible." Immediately, he pushed his tiramisù toward me. "I wish you'd eat some of this. . . ."

After a burial service in the late 1980s that Skip conducted as an U.S. Army Reserve chaplain near Camp Wauwepex, his Boy Scout camp on Long Island, and when his "boundaries were particularly thin," he stopped by the camp. Skip was, he said, "having a sort of breakdown in the delayed trauma of Vietnam. I was spiraling down in grief, biting my cheek. I was trying to get reconnected. I walked around and put cold water from the lake on my face and picked up a pinecone and I said to myself, Look at this pinecone. I'm not going to slip away. I still have the pinecone on my bureau at home."

He found peace and a new understanding of his priesthood by working at a senior center in the Bronx, not far from Hastings. "I had to pay the bills. I was a full-time senior center director and part-time parish priest. It was over the tables in the senior center that I realized how important it is to connect. When all is said and done, you have to show up.

"When you're trying to work up an SSI [Supplemental Social Security income] package for a senior who is hanging by her fingernails and she's in bad shape and you stay late to work that stuff up—you're the only guy in town. It's not like you're up at the altar saying [his voice became stentorian], 'The Lord be with you,' and just moving on. That experience—it's where the basic stuff is. As Jack Lax said, 'You need to love one another.' It's as simple as that."

The difference for Skip was that the Virginia congregation had "enormous expectations of what they wanted for themselves not only on a physical level but on a spiritual level. And if you tied yourself to that unfocused sense of things, you were bouncing all over the place." But at the senior center, the needs were defined and specific and he found "it was salvation for me."

In an additional effort to help himself reconnect with other people and with God, Skip took up centering prayer, a spiritual exercise that combines an aspect of Zen Buddhism with the teachings of the Trappist monk Thomas Keating as a way to get a fix on where God is. Rather than focusing concentration on a mantra or one's breathing, centering prayer relies more on intention than attention. By clearing one's mind of thought or emotion, the centering person is able to wait for God. Keating describes it as "two friends sitting in silence, just being in each other's presence." Skip says, "Again, you have to show up and intend to be part of the story. God is around us, trying to comment. You have to consent to being part of this greatness and allow God to be present. You can't dial this up; you have to be available and bring your guard down."

At first thought, it may seem odd that priests often do not feel part of worship when they are leading a service, but it makes sense that if their concentration is on their work—leading prayers, conducting the service, preaching the sermon—their spiritual openness is limited. I always feel at home in a church, entirely comfortable, because I know the place and the liturgy so well and also because I have no responsibilities when sitting in a pew. Skip echoes other priests I know when he says, "I don't feel as comfortable in a church as you. When in church, I feel I *should* pray. I have to go to work." Thus the calm that centering prayer gives him and why he is drawn to desolate places, where he finds a deep spirituality. He stays for a few days whenever possible at a retreat in the Sonoran Desert in Arizona, where he can quietly walk the wilderness trails.

It was in the wilderness, sometime in the mid-1980s, that Skip had a profound spiritual experience. He was with a U.S. Army Reserve unit at Twentynine Palms in the high Mojave Desert in California, and he took a solo excursion to nearby Joshua Tree National Park, a million acres of spectacularly odd-shaped rock formations, desert brush, and the primeval spiky trees that give the park its name. Beside a dirt road near a large boulder, he was on his knees, looking at flora, when he had "a sense of integration. I heard God say, 'I have always loved you.' And," he told me, laughing, "He didn't do it with an accent. It made me think, This is how Moses may have heard the voice in the burning bush."

These and other experiences derived from centering prayer helped make him the priest he hoped to be, and his abilities did not go unnoticed. Skip's work with the senior center caught the attention of Paul Moore, then the bishop of New York. The charismatic bishop liked this soldier-priest. The two became friends, and he asked Skip to be chair of the diocesan budget committee, which traditionally is the path to something bigger.

Skip's position in the U.S. Army Reserve led him to an assignment at the Pentagon for the six months of the first war in Iraq, in 1990–91. His experience with the budget committee showed he could organize complex issues, and that ability was put to use in confidential meetings at the United States Military Academy at West Point, in which he met with all branches of the armed services that deal with biologically or chemically contaminated human remains. Skip is a specialist in the pastoral care of casualties, and the report and guidelines he helped write were used in the Gulf War, and still are today.

Bishop Moore, who retired in 1989, was succeeded by Richard F. Grein. Skip found the two men quite different but equally influential on him. "Where Paul Moore was a leader through a delightful chaos, Dick Grein was well organized and hard to get close to, but he knew that and strived hard to overcome it. You couldn't help but feel a connection with that struggle on a deeper level—it mirrored my own. By some discrete portion, I am what I am today because of Dick Grein: his knowledge of the church, how to do things."

While my life to now may not have had the intense drama of Skip's, it has had the mundane but serious challenges and crises many of us experience. Ten years after Karen and I were married, my career stalled, and the financial worries it engendered also unleashed anxiety, insecurities, and anger we had each felt but not addressed. Divorce, which was anathema to my parents and had been to me as well, was suddenly a possibility. The Church and what remained of my faith provided no help; marriage counseling and psychotherapy did. Together and individually, we were able to confront and resolve our most corrosive issues. And without our two young sons ever saying a word, they contributed greatly. Growing up, Karen had several times felt the effect of divorce, and through her knowledge of what pain that would bring our children, I came to understand how important it was for us to do everything possible to stay together. Our shared love for our boys made us work even harder to find our way back to each other, which we did, and which made us stronger. We had both looked long enough to find the right person—I was thirty-eight when we married and Karen turned thirty on our honeymoon—and we joked that if we couldn't get it right with each other at our ages, we wouldn't manage any better with others.

I had not seen Skip for several years and we had fallen out of communication when I encountered him in an unlikely way. In 1992, the Most Reverend George Carey, the archbishop of Canterbury and head of the Anglican Communion, came to New York City. There was a reception for him, attended by many American bishops, at the Metropolitan Club on Fifth Avenue, an elaborate and sedate pile for the congregation of the establishment. Among those bishops was Harold Robinson, the priest my father was having lunch with all those years ago when Lauriston Scaife, the bishop of Western New York, came to San Diego to recruit Harold to go to Buffalo as the dean of St. Paul's Cathedral. Harold and his wife, Marie, took me in as I traveled through Buffalo to and from home while at Hobart College, and they became a second family to me, their four daughters the closest I have to sisters. Harold went on to become the bishop of Western New York, and was now retired, living in Manhattan and helping out in the Diocese of New York. In 1982, he married Karen and me at her grandmother's country home, in a living room largely full of Jews of various devotion. To our surprise, when the time came in the service for the Lord's Prayer, some could recite it from memory. (One, a fearful flier, found the prayer very useful.) And ten years later, when Karen and I hit that very tough patch in our marriage, Harold's counsel was invaluable—although his advice to me invoked not prayer but a reminder of the person he had known me to be throughout my life. He, Marie, and I had a dinner date after the reception for the archbishop. I went to meet them at the club. When I arrived and said whom I was looking for, rather than being shown a seat to wait, I was sent upstairs to the reception. In the sea of ecclesiastical purple shirts and white clerical collars, I could immediately discern that I was one of only a handful of people wearing a tie. But I was not uncomfortable. I'd spent my life around people like these. If anything, I found it a bit amusing.

Almost the first person I ran into as I swam through the crowd was Skip, in a black suit and black shirt to go with his white clerical collar, one of the few priests among so many bishops. I'm not sure which of us was more surprised. We greeted each other warmly and he told me that when Bishop Grein replaced Paul Moore in 1989, Grein had appointed him the canon to the ordinary for the Diocese of New York, which meant that he was the bishop's chief of staff and problem solver. We agreed to get together in quieter surroundings.

As I turned to continue my search for the Robinsons, the archbishop, the successor to Cranmer of the Book of Common Prayer, a tall, commanding white-haired figure with large thin-rimmed glasses, briskly walked up to me and demanded, "Who are *you?*"

He was not a figure to whom I ever expected to explain

myself. Now I *was* uncomfortable. For a good Episcopalian, being examined by the archbishop of Canterbury is only one step below Saint Peter asking for an account of your life at the Pearly Gates. I swallowed hard, said why I was there, and figured he would summon someone to throw me out. Instead, he asked, "What do you do?"

I told him I was a writer. He looked interested.

"What's your latest book?"

My latest book was the paperback edition of *Woody Allen: A Biography,* which had come out a couple of months earlier, just as Woody's breakup with Mia Farrow and new relationship with Soon-Yi Previn became fodder for every news outlet. Considering the notoriety and tabloid sensationalism of the story, I assumed the archbishop's reaction would be one of reproof. Instead, his face lighted up.

"Woody Allen? I quote him all the time! Does your book have a black-and-white photo of him on the cover?"

It does.

"I have it. It's wonderful," he said, and we talked for some time. I wished my father had been there to see this. (My mother loved the story when I recounted the event to her.) Not only would he have liked to meet the archbishop, the pure luck of the moment, as well as the irony of our exchange, would have amused him no end.

There was a service the next day at the Cathedral of St. John the Divine and Harold and Marie took me first to Bishop Grein's residence on the grounds and then with them to their seats in the choir stalls. The sight of the archbishop, who, dressed in his regal cope and miter and by force of personality, radiated an aura of ecclesiastical solemnity and power, made me feel connected in church in a way I had not felt for years.

Later, I went to see Woody, to ask if he would sign a copy of my biography that I could send along to England. He laughed at my recital of the conversation about it, picked up the book and pen I had brought, and immediately wrote:

Dear Archbishop,

Here's hoping you're right and I'm wrong.

All the best,
Woody Allen

I was a father twice over when Skip and I reunited. Simon was five, John two. Both had been baptized by the chaplain at the Episcopal Home in Los Angeles, where my mother had moved ten years earlier, and Karen and I took them regularly to All Saints', where they fidgeted in the pew and made losing yourself in the service almost impossible. My mother came for a weekend about once a month and we attended church together. Despite my growing doubts about faith, Karen and I wanted our kids to have a solid Episcopal background that would give them a sense not only of the family business but of a spiritual community and of something much greater than themselves; or at the very least, give them something to reject later in life. And while I had more and more trouble with the words of the Apostles' and Nicene Creeds and felt so much a hypocrite that often I would not join in the recitation of them or of the prayers that troubled me, I loved the music. Even the hymns with the most childish rhymes released an emotional charge that I have yet to understand, and sometimes the music would bring me to the verge of tears—perhaps because I was reminded of something I was losing, or perhaps just because music plays deeply on feeling.

The rector of All Saints', Carol Anderson, was among the first group of women to be officially ordained Episcopal priests, in January 1977. (An unsanctioned group was ordained in 1974.) The occasion was a great cause célèbre in the Anglican Communion and hardly a unanimous decision even within the Episcopal Church: The presiding bishop, John Allin, was among the traditionalists who believed that because none of Jesus' disciples was a woman, women should not be priests. (My mother agreed with him. Now the presiding bishop, the head of the Episcopal church, is a woman, Katherine Jefferts Schori.) I was assigned by *Esquire* magazine to write a story about the effect of this on the Church, and I interviewed Carol, among many others. She impressed me enormously with her intellect, her affability, and her obvious calling to the priesthood. Before women were ordained, it made no sense to me that they were excluded. The rationale that women couldn't be priests because none of the disciples was a woman made as much sense as banning scholars from the priesthood because none of the disciples was a scholar. Carol's attitude and presence made the change unassailably just and reasonable to me. She grew up the daughter of nominal Methodists who seldom went to church and considered herself a humanist until college courses in religion and work in the civil rights movement in the 1960s convinced her that something stronger was needed. In Kierkegaard she found someone who "looked into the face of evil and dread and came out with an understanding that was not fatalistic," as she put it in a *New York Times* story the day after her ordination. She knew what she was talking about: She herself had looked into the face of evil when two white supremacists set on her with baseball bats during a 1960s civil rights demonstration and severely damaged her knees. They were ready to do worse but fled when police appeared; Carol believes they would have killed her. The evil she saw in the hatred on their faces made her believe, like my father and Skip, that evil is a malevolent power.

The parish she was assigned to in New York—St. James, on Madison Avenue—was just down the block from my apartment and whenever I went to church it was there (Karen had attended as a child). At the first service I went to where she helped celebrate Communion, two priests served the Sacrament, each with half the rail to speed things along, and I crossed to the other side of the aisle when it was time to go to the altar so I could receive it from her. Then, proving again how small the world can be, ten years after Karen and I moved to Los Angeles, Carol was brought in as our new rector.

In 1993, my mother was diagnosed with amyotrophic lateral sclerosis (ALS, or Lou Gehrig's disease), a progressive neurodegenerative disease that affects nerve cells in the brain and the spinal cord and erodes their ability to initiate and control muscle movement. It is a slow, unrelenting disease, one that leaves the mind intact while day by day it walls away its victims. Imagine squirrels eating the covering on a telephone line, eventually short-circuiting it. That's what happens to the coating on the neurons: Day after day, a few more short out. First there is trouble with walking, then with arm movements, then with speech, then with breathing.

I went to see my mother several times a week, and in the last year of her life, nearly every day. It was torture for me to look on helplessly as she regressed from being able to speak to slurring to making no sound; from being able to write notes to barely scrawling them to only making lines on paper. But during that time, she expressed hope in the life ahead, in which she expected to be reunited with my father and to be with God. On one of the last days she could hold a pen, she shakily wrote down the hymns she wanted at her funeral. She seemed matter-of-fact about this as I read them back to her to be sure I had them right. My concentration on communicating with her buried my emotions, but when I got to my car, I felt the bottomless pit my stomach had turned to. It is an old cliché that the last lesson our parents teach us is how to die, but both my parents showed a level of grace that I hope I'll have.

One of my mother's greatest pleasures toward the end of her life was her relationship with the Reverend Anne Tumilty, then an All Saints' assistant rector who looked after the needs of the elderly. My mother's disapproval of women priests had been softened when, in the 1980s, a lifelong friend in Canada wrote to say she was called to the ministry, and it was banished by her time with Anne, whose pastoral care and devotion gave my mother companionship, comfort, and spiritual support.

On a Saturday morning in October 1995, a week before what was to be my mother's eighty-eighth birthday, a nurse at the home called to say she had refused breakfast and seemed determined to eat no more. Karen and I went to see her. She was weak but comfortable in her bed. She could move her eyes and she kept turning them toward a photo of my father in his clerical robes, next to the crucifix on her wall. I'm going to be with him, she seemed to say. She continued to refuse meals, and the next day, small doses of morphine were begun to keep her comfortable.

Anne heard what was happening and suggested we have a bedside service. In eight short services, the Book of Common Prayer takes the faithful through the whole of life, and the Visitation of the Sick is in its place after Holy Baptism, Offices of Instruction, the Order of Confirmation, the Form of Solemnization of Matrimony, the Thanksgiving of Women after Child-birth, and before the Communion of the Sick and the Burial of the Dead. My mother was either deeply asleep or in a coma as we sat by her bed. Using my father's red leather-bound 1928 prayer book, which she kept by her bedside, we said the Lord's Prayer and then, responsively,

> *O Lord, save thy servant;*
> *Who putteth her trust in thee;*
> *Send her help from thy holy place;*
> *And evermore mightily defend her;*
> *Let the enemy have no advantage of her;*
> *Nor the wicked approach to hurt her;*
> *Be unto her, O Lord, a strong tower;*
> *From the face of her enemy;*

O Lord, hear our prayer.
And let our cry come unto thee.

Anne read several other prayers, then, when we came
to "A Prayer for a Sick Person, when there appeareth but
small hope of Recovery," she asked me to read it aloud. "O
Father of mercies, and God of all comfort, our only help
in time of need; We fly unto thee for succour in behalf of
this thy servant, here lying in great weakness of body," I
began, my voice catching after the first few words. "Look
graciously upon her, O Lord. . . ." I had to stop, as I began
to sob and could not catch my breath. It took several minutes for me haltingly to finish the last seven lines of the
prayer. At the end, I felt I had handed her over to a God she
was ready to meet and I doubted existed, and I was left
with a mixture of sadness and guilt along with a huge sense
of loss, not only now of both parents but of the faith we
had so deeply and easily shared.

My mother never regained consciousness. I spent a
good part of the next two days in her room, hoping to be
with her at the end, but went home each night. Karen and
I were still asleep very early the third morning when a
nurse called to say my mother had peacefully died.

She was cremated and her funeral was in the Episcopal
Home chapel, where she had worked nearly every day on
the altar guild, preparing for the various services. A photo
of her taken by the chaplain was at the door. In it, she is
lighting the altar candles with a three-foot-long wooden-
handled candle lighter that curls at the top like a ram's
horns, with a lighted wick on one side and on the other a

brass bell-shaped damper for snuffing out the flames at the end of the service. Her face is concentrated on the job, but she looks utterly at peace as well.

Following a memorial service at St. Alban's for her many friends who still worshiped there, there was a reprise of the trip to Camp Stevens with my father's ashes nineteen years before. It was another beautiful fall day. The chapel was unchanged, but the trees beside the pool had run their life span and been replaced by others; the prevailing wind still carries the leaves into the pool. The camp director and his wife, who have fulfilled and exceeded the dreams my father had for the place, were (and are) still there, as were many of the same mourners who had come for my father. Once again, Boone Sadler recited the simple service, and once again he and I each dug a hand into the bag of ashes and cast them behind the chapel. But Happy the dog was long dead, and this time there was no leaping after them.

What leaped out instead was the comfort and love of Karen and our boys, the grandchildren my father never met. They were eight and five, too young to really understand what we had done that day. But Karen and I weren't. We talked about whether I wanted my ashes scattered here, as well. We recently recounted that day, and I'm glad of it, for many reasons, not least because she thought that I said I did and I thought I said I didn't.

John became a regular camper and through high school returned for a week or two each summer as a counselor. He always paid a visit to his grandparents. The chapel and many of the older buildings and about one-quarter of the trees at the camp were destroyed in a forest fire in 2007, but there was good insurance and there are many dedicated supporters who are helping to rebuild. The bronze plaque with the names of my parents and half a dozen others whose families liked what my father started and had ashes of their loved ones scattered behind the chapel survived; it will be affixed to the wall of the replacement. I'm on the board of the camp now, not only because Karen and I have had the good fortune to help it financially but for obvious emotional reasons. I serve with pleasure but also with some guilt and and a touch of shame about my lapsed faith. Only the camp director among my fellow members—several of them priests, another a pal from my earliest days there, all of them devout—knows of my struggles. I go there because I love the place and because it honors the memory of my father—one of the buildings is Lax-Sadler Lodge. On each visit, I remember the astronomer by the campfire and the services in the chapel and the quiet Friday nights, along with my other experiences both mundane and raucous. I am reminded of who I was, and I look to connect that person to who I have become.

As for my ashes, a *few* will be scattered at Camp Stevens.

Eight

Bishop Packard in Baghdad, following an
Ash Wednesday retreat with chaplains,
helping Chaplain Reese Hutcheson
with his bulletproof vest

After my mother died, I had no reason to fake faith and hide my doubts and concerns. As emotionally difficult as it was to admit, it no longer seemed plausible to me that Christ is the Redeemer sent by God to save the souls within the ectoplasm and stardust that is humankind. (Just typing that heretical sentence brings a chill, as it reminds me of a time when it would have been more than enough to have me burned alive at the stake.) Even though I still find His example worth following, and try to do it, that is a far step removed from where I started. This fracture from the core of my parents' faith left me with the feeling that I had betrayed them, and although it also made me feel personally incomplete and parentally irresponsible toward Simon and John about educating them in faith and passing on a family legacy that had been a great guide in my life, I could find no alternative. Really, though, I didn't want one. What I wanted was to have what I'd always had, but the faith I had accepted without question and could articulate by catechismal rote could not be recaptured in reverse. Words may define an inward and spiritual feeling, but they cannot create one.

I know that faith ought to be the result of a singular journey that allows God into one's heart, but it was a journey for which I could find no path. In a further step back from spirituality, I began to feel the greater loss in this was not my relationship with God, whose existence, at least in a personal sense, was now doubtful, but with my father, whose existence was never in doubt, whose faith withstood many challenges, and whose example has been my guide even as I have veered away.

Meanwhile, although Skip's path has been a winding one—and I would say the better for it—he has grown in faith in the course of a ministry with far more varied responsibilities than that of most clerics. He spent seven years as canon to the ordinary for the Diocese of New

York, handling problems of every stripe for his bishop. Such a job demands executive and political savvy more than it requires pastoral care, and after so many years of it, he was all too aware the work "pulls you away from people." In 1996, he asked if he could be sent to a parish so he could be more personally engaged, and the Church of the Epiphany on Manhattan's Upper East Side called him as their interim priest in charge. It was a parish with conflict among its members and it needed a calm presence. Skip provided the calm, and he would later be asked to do the same thing for a parish in suburban Rye, New York. But while he was able to make better relationships in his pastoral life, his marriage finally dissolved, leaving two daughters—one in high school, the other a recent college graduate—split between parents. Skip remains close to both.

Whether the root cause of the breakup was Vietnam, the post-traumatic stress, or a combination of those and other problems, he is not sure. What he does say is that several times in his life, stress or crisis propelled him closer to God and to his pastoral work, and the divorce marked the fourth time this had happened. The first was the silence he experienced and came to understand in seminary, which convinced him he was on the path meant for him. The struggles at the large Virginia parish, which led to his virtually rebooting his ministry at Hastings-on-Hudson, triggered the second instance. His work at the senior center was, he says, "an *ah-ha* moment," when pastoral work was reduced to its essence of simply being on hand to help someone when no one else was there, and he felt the essential need for him as a person, regardless of the priesthood, to connect to people. The pain of his divorce was mitigated a couple of years later when he met Brook Hedick, a musician, composer, and educator with an interest in Christian formation, who had a young daughter, Clara, whom Skip has adopted. They married in 1999.

Skip and I fell out of contact again in the mid-1990s. After Skip went to the Church of the Epiphany, a mutual friend told me that Skip's parish was only a few blocks from where for many years I had lived in New York and where this friend still lived. My visits to New York then were always short, and while I told our friend that I intended to call Skip on one of them, I never did. Guilt held me back. This was the period, after my mother's death, when I really pulled away from the Church, and I didn't want to tell him or even talk it over.

Then in 2000, I had a call from Skip. He had been elected Episcopal Bishop Suffragan for the Armed Forces, Federal Institutions, and Chaplaincies, which meant that rather than oversee a diocese, he would be in charge of all Episcopalians in the armed forces around the world, in federal prisons, and in Veterans Affairs facilities. He asked me to be among his personal party at his ordination at the National Cathedral in Washington, D.C.

There was a small dinner in a room at the cathedral in Skip's honor the night before his consecration. The group included several bishops and priests and Skip's family and friends. After a lifetime of ease in such settings, I felt the odd man out, largely because of my diminished faith, which I hid that night.

At the majestic service the next morning, the cathedral, a resplendent example of Gothic architecture built over the last century, was filled, and sixteen bishops were gathered in the chancel. To the booming accompaniment of the pipe organ and the singing of the hymn "Christ Is Made the Sure Foundation" ("Christ the head and cornerstone / Chosen of the Lord, and precious / Binding all the Church in one"), bishops and priests and a choir processed past the pews in the nave to the chancel. Skip made the promise required by the liturgy: "In the name of the Father, and of the Son, and of the Holy Spirit, I, George Elden Packard, chosen Bishop of the Church for the Armed Forces, Federal Institutions, and Chaplaincies, solemnly declare that I do believe the Holy Scriptures of the Old and New Testaments to be the Word of God, and to contain all things necessary to salvation; and I do solemnly engage to conform to the doctrine, discipline and worship of the Episcopal Church." After the congregation, which included a contingent from his former parish in Virginia, affirmed that it was our will that Skip be ordained a bishop and that we would uphold him in his work, the presiding bishop of the Episcopal church questioned him regarding his calling to this position and reminded him, "Your heritage is the faith of patriarchs, prophets, apostles and martyrs, and those of every generation who have looked to God in hope. Your joy will be to follow him who came, not to be served, but to serve, and to give his life for the ransom." There followed seven questions: "Will you accept this call and fulfill this trust to the obedience of Christ?" ("I will obey Christ, and will serve His name," Skip replied.) "Will you be faithful in prayer and in the study of the Holy Scripture, that you may have the mind of Christ?" ("I will, for He is my help.") "Will you boldly proclaim and interpret the Gospel of Christ, enlightening the minds and stirring up the conscience of your people?" ("I will in the power of the Spirit.") "As chief priest and pastor, will you encourage and support all baptized people in their gifts of ministries, nourish them from the riches of God's grace, pray for them without ceasing, and celebrate with them the sacraments of our redemption?" ("I will, in the name of Christ, the Shepherd and Bishop of our souls.") "Will you guard the faith, unity, and discipline of the Church?" ("I will, for the love of God.") "Will you share with your fellow bishops in the government of the whole Church; will you sustain your fellow presbyters and take counsel with them; will you guide and strengthen the deacons and all the others who minister in the Church?" ("I will, by the grace given me.") "Will you be merciful to all, show compassion to the poor and strangers, and defend those who have no helper?" ("I will, for the sake of Jesus Christ.")

This stateliness was regularly interrupted by loud hiccups from six-year-old Clara, who had lined up her Beanie Babies on the rail beyond her front-row pew so they could see the service. "This is the best affirmation of the Holy Spirit's playfulness I can think of," Skip recalled with a laugh years later. "It's a reminder not to take all this too seriously. Liturgy should not be a ball and chain. It should open us to the limitless possibilities that are in life."

In the holiest moment of the service, the sixteen bishops laid their hands upon Skip's head and he became one of them. Skip put on his new ecclesiastical vestments. He had now stepped into the unbroken two-thousand-year-long line of apostolic descendants, and taken his place with Bishops Augustine and Thomas à Becket, Cranmer and George Carey, as well as his mentors Paul Moore and Richard Grein. The congregation gave him lengthy and enthusiastic applause. He looked great, as was my pleasure for him. But I also felt that while our parallel lives during the Vietnam years were at odds, in matters of faith they were now even more so.

Skip was eighteen months into his job when the World Trade towers were destroyed on September 11, 2001. A few hours after the attack, he learned that some of his armed forces and hospital chaplains had been deployed at Ground Zero, and dressed in the black shirt and white clerical collar that are the uniform of a priest (he prefers to be identified that way), he made his way from his office in the Episcopal Church Center at Second Avenue and Forty-third Street in Manhattan, the headquarters for the Church in the United States, to the devastation. It was still raining ashes, and steam rose from the pile. His federal identification got him past checkpoints.

Skip had with him a few useful priestly things, including a stole, which he wore as he blessed the few remains of the dead that were being recovered from the rubble. Like Skip and all the others who toiled there, the stole soon was covered in the dust from the wreckage, which included, he says, "The incinerated souls from the doomed towers." Skip gave the stole to Bishop Mark Sisk of the Diocese of New York to wear at a memorial service in the overflowing Cathedral of St. John the Divine a few days after the attack.

Skip took over the site for the Church as chaplains and other workers were brought in from around the country. The gateway to the perimeter of the ruins was through St. Paul's Chapel, opposite the east side of the World Trade Center. (The chapel, part of Trinity Episcopal Church on Wall Street, became the center for the relief effort.) The work was hard, gory, and had echoes of Vietnam.

"At the pile—soon to be the pit—at Ground Zero," he recalled, "in the field morgue they presented us with hardly enough to be called a body, but they were bagged in solemn silence and dignity." In an attempt to provide psychological relief for the workers, a critical debriefing team was brought in, but never used. As Skip knew well from his experiences on ambush and patrol, the sensory overload of such experience numbs emotion. He was there for three months.

He spent another year supporting the Church's response in the aftermath of Hurricane Katrina in 2005, while (as he had after 9/11) still attending to his other duties, which included trips to Iraq, military bases in the United States and abroad, and Micronesia—irony of ironies, it fell under his purview; we hope to make a visit there together.

Then Skip was struck by a series of his own natural disasters. A CT scan in 2005 to monitor possible effects on his kidneys because of high blood pressure showed two malignant tumors in one of them. He recovered well from the surgery but the following year was diagnosed with prostate cancer, which he views as his fifth spiritual awakening. At the same time, he "started to get a little more sober about my longevity."

Skip had successful prostate surgery, but in late 2007 the cancer returned. This discovery coincided with a sabbatical he had long looked forward to and was about to take. Rather than travel, reflect, and otherwise have a break from the stress of his work, however, he had to stay in New York for forty-two days of radiation. Skip built his days around his hour-long visits to Memorial Sloan-Kettering Cancer Center in Manhattan. He began them between 5:00 and 6:00 a.m. with thirty minutes of centering prayer in his living room. Then he rode the train from his home to the city and spent a couple of hours reading, writing, and keeping up with e-mail, and went to the hospital for his daily 11:00 a.m. appointment. Afterward there was a workout. When he returned home in the late afternoon, he spent another twenty minutes in centering prayer.

We had been in better touch for the past year or so. I was in New York a couple of weeks after his radiation began and asked if I could accompany him to the hospital, figuring a friend might be a support. I was happy that he said yes. It was two weeks before Christmas. He was wearing dark green khakis, a flannel shirt, an overcoat, and a baseball cap. He was outwardly calm and full of his usual wry humor. The waiting room was pleasantly sterile, with chairs and sofas and a view outside. It didn't surprise me that after only a dozen visits, Skip knew practically all the staff and patients and that he had a word for each, and they for him. He was acting as a chaplain to his fellow patients, listening every day to their stories and fears but not pressing prayers on them. His own spirits obviously held up: To celebrate his thirtieth day of radiation and the new year, he wore a necktie (and his usual socks) as his otherwise-naked body was bombarded.

We corresponded a good deal by e-mail in the following weeks. In an effort to try to understand centering prayer, I immersed myself in books by Thomas Keating and even the daily spiritual exercises prescribed by Ignatius Loyola, which Skip had recommended to me. I could never get comfortable as I did this. I think the reason is twofold. It was hard to try to connect with a presence I really didn't think was there—I felt like someone fiddling with a Ouija board. And conversely, if I *had* connected, it would have scared the hell out of me.

In an e-mail to Skip, after inquiring about his health and spirits, I said, "I've been spending a lot of time with Keating. It's hard going but very good. I realize that my fear is, whom will I encounter in centered prayer? What if I find God? What if I find myself? Are these people I want to come face-to-face with?"

"I've been afraid of the same thing," he replied, "but then God has gently (but insistently) nudged me in my waking life and in my dreams. Centering prayer isn't the sole channel. This is actually a win-win, I think, because whether you greet God or the Self, you will still achieve peace . . . which is God's ultimate gift to you."

We met again in person in February 2008, shortly after the radiation ended, and I asked him what effect this illness had had on his faith. Skip doesn't believe much happens by coincidence, and he related one event that deeply affected him. After leaving Memorial Sloan-Kettering following his twenty-first radiation treatment, he "thought it would be a hoot to get some MSK stuff from the gift shop—it's not everybody who has Sloan-Kettering boxers," but to get to that part of the hospital meant going by a different route, which took him by the entrance to St. Catherine of Siena Roman Catholic Church, operated by Dominican fathers.

"Seeing the church surprised me and spoke to my concerns about where Jesus' companionship was in this illness," he said, and he found himself drawn inside. "I was having a lot of trouble re-creating my prayer time in the city, but the Spirit presented a way. There is a huge Jesus at St. Catherine's, His toes worn off by people touching them after Mass. It gave me a sense of: Jesus died like this, it was awful, and there's hope." Skip remains acutely aware of all that he has done in his life, especially in Vietnam, and he is often reminded of a verse in Psalm 25: "Remember not the sins of my youth, nor my transgressions; according to thy mercy remember thou me for thy goodness' sake, O Lord."

"You need Christ when you are fully aware of your sins," he went on. "In prayer I say I know I am under judgment. One time I heard a small voice say, What a grim reaper you are, and I thought to myself [he laughed], I'm screwed. But the connecting tissue is that in many of the collects [a different prayer each week, said before the reading of the Epistle] there is Jesus standing between God's judgment and me, and all of us. There is a verse of a hymn that I always think of: 'Intercessor, Friend of sinners, Earth's Redeemer, plead for me.' [It is in the third verse of

"Alleluia! Sing to Jesus."] If I have a tombstone, I would like on it 'Jesus, friend of sinners, plead for me.' "

It seemed to me as he said this that he knew he was forgiven by God but not by himself.

"Absolutely," he said. "It's probably the biggest sin—that you don't forgive yourself. The people I've killed . . ." He paused and shook his head. "You've led your life with such high expectations—and part of older age is wisdom and realizing that [he laughed] lower expectations are smarter, based on the resources you have. But also, you can't live up to all the promises you've made, though you should try to. You need some entity in the universe to make up the difference. I think particularly that verse in that hymn shows how we just need an advocate. That's why, when somebody said about Woody that he must be terribly lonely, I don't perceive the man to be lonely. But as you enter your death without some expectation, that seems like a lonely thought."

Later he casually asked me, "Who do you expect to see in the thirty seconds after you die?"

No one, I said. I expect it to be lights-out. My mother was so sure she was going to see my father, and they both expected to meet God, as I did for a long time. Skip nodded his head but said nothing. We were coming to the end of a nearly three-hour conversation and moved on in our wrap-up. A few minutes after I left his office, I realized I hadn't asked him what he expected, and sent him an e-mail doing so.

His answer was only slightly less Delphic than my father's Kleenex response: "I expect to meet people and not necessarily the ones I prefer. All good, though." (On another occasion, Skip said, "God is no Kleenex, and neither is He a cocker spaniel playfully tugging at your napkin." Another conundrum to unravel.)

Skip and I met again not long after this exchange. It was Ascension Day and we needed to finish in time for him to attend the service in the chapel of the Episcopal Church Center. In passing, he offered his interpretation for the day's importance. I think my father would have loved it:

"On a purely functional basis, the Church had to move Jesus and His risen appearance out of the moment so Pentecost could occur. How can the Spirit come down if Jesus is appearing at every garage sale? The Kingdom of God is at hand when we're awakened to the Christ in each other."

Several times in our conversations, Skip and I have puzzled over the turns our lives in faith have taken. "When we were at Hobart," I said one day, "I felt a real connection to God, that He had my calling card and knew my name. Did you?"

"No," he replied. "I've always sensed that you had that. How come you don't know where it is? What happened? Did you somehow pass this card to me under the table?"

I wish I knew.

When I was losing my faith, it took some time for me to realize it. I wasn't looking to lose it; I just suddenly noticed there was a separation I had never known. I was like a car whose tires all have imperceptible leaks. Everything runs smoothly, until suddenly four flats bring you to a halt. Faith, I guess, is like love: It withers when unattended. Through my late twenties and early thirties, I took mine for granted. Then when my father died, my anchor slipped, and I began to wonder about a God who seems to play spiritual hide-and-seek. My inward and spiritual feeling had in part been overrun by what I saw as the external and base manifestations of faith. Without my father's example and force of personality to bolster me, the concerns that fueled my earlier, transient doubts now solidified: the surety by so many that God is on their side; the political and social narrative drowned out by the shrill of fundamentalism; the fact that virtually every religion has limited or still limits equal rights for women, has supported slavery or still condones injustices, and is heterosexual-centric; the daily reports of one murderous outrage or another committed in the name of whatever the deity; the contemplation of the words in the services that I knew by heart but now, looked at one by one, did not make the sense they used to; and the overall feeling that religion is carrot and stick. My lifelong security that what I believed was true now was all too black and white: Believe this and have eternal life through the Savior, who died for your sins. Wherever I looked, the answer of faith seemed to be, This way or no way.

Which raised another problem: In one way or another, every religion offers sanctuary in the afterlife, or an eternal life better than the one you have now—if you follow its rules. Attractive a notion as that is, I began to feel like a bounty hunter, doing something for the reward. But I also found the essential tenet of Christianity (and Judaism, for that matter) attractive and meaningful: Love one another; love your neighbor as yourself; do unto others as you would have them do unto you. You don't love someone because you want her to love you back or because you will otherwise profit; you love her because she makes you feel whole and her love makes you better. And in simplest terms, this made me feel that we make our own heaven and hell on Earth by the way we choose to act. Behave well, not from fear of punishment in another life, but because living an honorable and caring life is a personal reward of its own that also makes community life better. If we act only in self-interest and without fear of reprisal, daily life will be chaos. And it often is chaos because members of one religion or another have been willing to shoot, bomb, or otherwise kill in the name of their God. Sectarianism has diminished the Creator of all that is seen and unseen to a tribal totem concerned only about the well-being and interests of true believers, no matter the cost to whoever is not Us. How can God be great if God is made so provincial?

Of course, the outcome of religious faith is often positive. The feeling of spiritual community a parish offers brings peace to millions of decent people. The sacred music of Gregorian chants, hymns, Mozart's Requiem touches something deep inside; the art, often at once beautiful and brutal in its depictions of suffering, burrows into the imagination; the tradition of ritual and prayer gives a sense of continuity over millennia; the architecture of great cathedrals reminds worshipers that there is something much greater than they, while an intimate chapel surrounds the faithful with a sense that it is something they are a part of. All express the idea of the holy and mankind's desire to be part of it.

Every day as I walk to and from my office, I pass three

churches within two blocks: Roman Catholic, Presbyterian, and my nominal parish, All Saints'. With other churches and the local synagogue, they alternate feeding the homeless; Monday is the day for All Saints' and each week 150 or more needy show up and are given a good meal and whatever fellowship they want. The selfless good that religion offers is broadly evident in programs such as these and in relief charities funded by the Catholic and Episcopal churches that respond to natural disasters with money that goes directly to help rather than to pay high overhead. All this is the real Christian behavior laid out in Matthew 25:35–36: "For I was hungry and you gave me food, I was thirsty and you gave me something to drink, I was a stranger and you welcomed me, I was naked and you gave me clothing, I was sick and you took care of me, I was in prison and you visited me."

My doubts are not unfamiliar ones, of course. Still, later in life than most, I was (and am) continuing to try to find my own accommodation with dogma. I started to question because I want to hold a belief, however uneven and contradictory, that I have found in my heart after a spiritual journey, rather than the tidy package I had comfortably accepted whole.

In "Peter Quince at the Clavier," Wallace Stevens wrote that "music is feeling, then, not sound." Faith, too, can be said to be feeling, not words, but that was not how I understood it. I had based my faith on words that defined what I believed, and in doing so, I locked that belief in a box. The challenge of faith is to use the words to lead you to the silence of deeper feeling. I've tried but been unable to find that feeling. When the words of belief became hollow because the specificity of dogma became untenable to me, the acceptance of a God who is interested in me, and the path to that God through Jesus Christ, which was the central tenet of my faith, disappeared.

That night at Camp Stevens when I was ten or eleven and the visiting astronomer waved his hand across the expanse of the starry sky and recited from Psalm 19, "The heavens declare the glory of God; / and the firmament showeth his handy-work," gave me my first sense of the indescribable greatness of God, or whatever you want to call the organizer of the cosmos. Saint Anselm provided that handy definition: a being greater than which nothing can be conceived. But although Anselm would argue that because I can conceive of a God interactive in our life, He must exist, I also can conceive of winning the lottery, which doesn't mean I will.

Now when I gaze at the stars and consider their untold number and the infinite universe in which all I see is less than a speck of the whole, I am at once in awe and made queasy by its unfathomable magnitude. When I fly at night and look at the countless lights of New York or Chicago or Los Angeles—every one the illumination of a street, a store, a home, a car, a symbol of a person—my insignificance overwhelms me and I am reminded that we each are the background, the anonymous extras in everyone else's life, and all that is below me is simply a bigger version of an anthill. I can imagine God, a prime mover, the organizing force, but that does not make Him, Her, or It a conscious force in human life. I am sympathetic to the notions of Einstein and the seventeenth-century philosopher Baruch Spinoza, ostracized from the Amsterdam Sephardic community at age twenty-four by writ of *cherem,* the highest Jewish ecclesiastical censure, for his naturalistic view of God. As Einstein summed it up in a 1929 telegram to Rabbi Herbert S. Goldstein, who had telegraphed Einstein to ask whether he believed in God: "I believe in Spinoza's God who reveals himself in the orderly harmony of what exists, not in a God who concerns himself with the fates and actions of human beings." And he added in a later essay, "The World as I See It":

The most beautiful experience we can have is the mysterious. It is the fundamental emotion that stands at the cradle of true art and true science. Whoever does not know it and can no longer wonder, no longer marvel, is as good as dead, and his eyes are dimmed. It was the experience of mystery—even if mixed with fear—that engendered religion. A knowledge of the existence of something we cannot penetrate, of the manifestations of the profoundest reason and the most radiant beauty—it is this knowledge and this emotion that constitute the truly religious attitude; in this sense, and in this alone, I am a deeply religious man.

Strange to say, I may not have come to such odds between the faith that took me well into my thirties and my lack of it now without the Vietnam War, which forced me to declare what I believed. All the thought, soul-searching, and writing that went into my CO statement became the foundation for my faith going forward, and the ingredients that went into it came from my store of child-hood conviction. As the years went by and brought new experiences and challenges, that untested foundation crumbled. Without the war, I could well have continued to sail along in my contented belief, in part because I never knew anything different and was not challenged to defend it. It is entirely possible that I would have accepted the offer of one of the bishops willing to sponsor me in semi-nary. Of course, I don't know what would have become of my faith once I delved into the course work, but I would have entered feeling I was on a solid footing with God. Perhaps I would have held so tightly to that feeling that I would have come out the kind of platitudinous priest my father abhorred.

Skip and I were talking about sermons the day he won-dered if I had passed him my calling card, and how my father noticed in his retirement that so many priests had no idea about what they were saying. Skip said he often sees the same thing.

"Not long ago, a priest said to me—he was completely serious, utterly serious—without guile, 'I think I'm called to the episcopacy, I'm called to be a bishop.' I thought to myself, Holy crap. He's barely thirty-four. I said, 'I think you're called to service.'

"These are just naïve things, like me asking you to come to Virginia and preach profound things about being in Micronesia and tell me about the little brown-skinned kids. Really, it's coming to people with the wrong question. You ask them, Where are you now? What's happening to you now? What of the Spirit is impacting you now? That is the thing that carries the day. The sermons that are good are the ones where you leave yourself and enter into a conversation: This is something that earnestly bothers me and I've wrestled with it and, *aha,* I've found this and it seems like it really makes sense, and it sizzles, don't you think? And the congregation vibrates with it, too, and you have that kind of moment that the Ignatians talk about; you have this environment of special discovery. It must have been the way Jesus intended it to be. But you seldom get a chance to enjoy a sermon for the devotional thing it is. The devotional thing is in the wrestling with it, not necessarily in the delivery. Sermon delivery is supposed to be haphazard. There are times I'm seeing people connected and that their lives have changed. Other times, they're dead-eyed. But in all instances we have a genuine hunger these days for being in places that are real."

On Sundays when he's home, Skip generally does not go to the Episcopal church where his wife, Brook, works, because a bishop's presence is distracting. Instead, he often goes to a nearby church, whose pastor he admires for his sermons.

"He preaches a sermon for about twenty minutes and then says, 'Why don't we all go up there around the altar and see what happens,' " Skip explained one day. "It's a very interesting way to think of life. It's really the question of what matters. He just invites people into the search with him."

Virtually every bishop works in formal surroundings:

There is usually an elaborate cathedral that is his seat, and when he goes to parishes, the services are made more elaborate by his presence. But Skip is the opposite. He has no cathedral; most of his services are done in mess tents in often difficult and dangerous surroundings. The result for him is a disconnect with traditional Episcopal worship, because as a soldier, and now as a bishop, his place of worship was and is makeshift. After more than thirty-five years, he finds it harder and harder to square how he con ducts his more ad hoc ministry with the standard rituals of the Church.

"Maybe it's because the surroundings for the services I take are usually so different, the Episcopal worship kind of closes me down," he went on. "A lot of the Episcopal worship today is overdeveloped and sterile, though that's not entirely true. Some places are more engaged and involve all generations. But for the most part, people sit in rows and they are told what to do, when to stand, when to sit, and so forth. Certain parts of the Episcopal liturgy make it seem we're kind of in lockstep, doing stuff by rote, like fund-raising for the organ, and people have to say their prayers for it. I'm finding the more festooned the liturgy is, the less valuable it is. My experiences at the retreat I go to in Arizona and in private centering prayer and other moments seem richer than that. The idea is to get together and affirm our mutual wonder about the mystery of God, to be there and be open in the moment, not uptight."

In many ways, Skip has come to sound much like my father did in his mid-sixties, shortly after he retired: a bit dismayed by his cohorts, grumpy about his Church in general, and hoping for a bit of peace with his God. Priests rehearse liturgy so much that they cannot always protect against losing their own spirituality in the performance of it. "What is meant to be the sweetness of spirit can become handcuffs for some" is how Skip puts it. He says, not entirely joking, that when he retires, he thinks he would like to work in a Home Depot store.

"Think of it. I work there and I put on my apron and they get to know me as this kind of squirrelly guy down aisle seven who is some sort of an authority on plumbing phalanges. I admire those guys. I'd like to do some writing and also be available to Sloan-Kettering or whatever hospice would have me. One of the reasons I want to go to Home Depot is that I think I'll meet more of the people I met in the radiation suites than I meet in church.

"And I've thought about us," he said. "How are these two trains passing each other? We start out at the same station, but are we going in the same direction? I started out resolutely Episcopalian and am becoming less denominational—"

"And," I interrupted, "I started out resolutely Episcopalian and went off the tracks."

To which he said, kindly and with a sudden trace of tears, "I've noticed this before during this project: I worry that I'm the doppelgänger in the story and our relationship has become a plot point. If you were to get some faith now, I would get the willies. You'd stop being the inquisitive horse's ass you are. You'd stop being the Eric I love, and, if you'll allow me, God loves." Then he added, "But being perpetually inquisitive and restless gives *you* no rest.

It's a predicament for those around you. You know, you deserve to have a hunch about God not based on anybody but yourself."

I laughed about being a horse's ass and in doing so demonstrated I am one, because blinded by his affectionate description of me, I missed the point of his concern and the cause for his brief tears. Over the several previous months, I'd pestered him for more information, for clarifications on things he'd said to me. I sometimes behaved more like a writer intent on tying up every loose end so I could finish a project than I did a friend. My feelings of camaraderie and love for him, which deepened even more in the eighteen-month course of our conversations about faith and our lives, were unthinkingly hidden by my professional concerns. Which sure limns the difference in how each of us goes about his work: A priest asks, Does your constant questioning interfere with your ability to connect not only with God but with those who love you? A writer asks, Do you have a sermon I can quote?

It took a good twenty-four hours for what he asked to sink in. Then I wrote to him that he was neither a doppelgänger nor a plot point. It is true that as young men we started on the road of faith from the same place and there's an undeniably convenient asymmetry to our travels since then that makes for useful tension between two people in a story. But I added that having reconnected with him on so profound a level, I could never trivialize him, and that what he had shared with me was useful for my enterprise but vital to my life.

Now in his mid-sixties and after several debilitating illnesses, Skip has to husband his strength so that he can put himself into what he preaches. The reward for him is not in what he says but how he came to say it.

"I find now when I do visitations as a bishop in all my regalia that I have panic attacks because I worry whether or not I'll have the stamina to do a sermon and then realize during it that I do—but there have been occasions when I don't. I've had four or five operations and so sometimes I've found myself avoiding services. Then I realized that I may be avoiding them because there's a kind of falseness that doesn't allow me to enter into the service. That's a terribly selfish thing. I have to tell myself, Get a hold of yourself, George."

He knows the percentages aren't in his favor for having a normal life span. He is blunt in his assessment of his future and completely uncomplaining.

"I don't know how many days I've got," he said one morning. We were talking in the conference room near his office. He was in his purple shirt and white collar, a baseball cap on his head to cut the glare of the overhead lights. He had just returned from a trip to a military base in Sicily during Holy Week. "I don't expect to be snapping towels in the locker room when I'm eighty. I'm trying to be mindful of the things that happen.

"I'm not trying to be a cowboy," he assured me. "I'll give you an example. A pickpocket took my wallet on the subway in Rome. Holy Saturday. Everybody was up in arms. I said, 'Ah, it doesn't matter.' A woman was taking us to the police, and my wife said, 'You're not really into this, are you?' And I answered, 'Look, I was in Vietnam and have had a couple of cancers. Why are we wasting the one full day we have in Rome screwing around with this?' I'm not trying to applaud my calmness, because other times I can be as nuts as the next person. But in this case, I thought, This is the direct result of practicing mindfulness."

I asked Skip how his illnesses affected his prayer life.

"I was doing centering prayer already, but I probably intensified it and worked on the Ignatian exam to find where I was with God and where He was with me in this moment." (He was referring to the five-step meditation developed by Ignatius Loyola: Recall that you are in the presence of God; look over your day with gratitude for this day's gifts; ask God to send His Holy Spirit to help you look honestly at your actions and attitudes and motives; a review of your day; a heart-to-heart talk with Jesus.)

One of Skip's best friends in the military, a rising star assumed by all who knew him to be on his way to admiral, recently died from ocular melanoma. Skip performed his funeral service. The two friends had often talked about their afflictions, and asked each other, "What the hell is this supposed to mean?"

I reminded Skip of his dismay forty-five years ago, when he asked how God could allow such a senseless tragedy as an avalanche of coal slag to wipe out a school full of children. He shook his head and said how naïve he had been. Despite all he has seen and what has happened to him, despite all the things that might make one question God's motives and mercy, he said asking that is looking for the wrong answer.

"It's the theodicy question," he said. "Why does God let

evil things happen? I think the focus has to be on what we do, rather than what it appears that God does. I'd be more cautious about even asking a question like that. I just try to keep my eye on what Jesus did in His life. He suffered and was pulled forward in history into something else in Easter. I think it's a luxury for people to sit back and draw their hand over their chins like I'm doing now [he laughed] and ask questions like, Why did God do this to me? I still get calls from this guy I met at Sloan-Kettering. His treatment's not gone well and I know he's just railing against it and against God, too. And there is the opposite of that—being the weeping puppy. God doesn't want you to whine. He wants you to stand upright and lean into what's before you, whatever it is—whether it's painful or challenging or good and joyous—and to live life in its fullness. Life in its fullness has its debits and credits. If it had all one thing, life would limp a little bit.

"When I talk with someone in the lounge at the radiation suite on the fourth floor of Sloan-Kettering and he's worried, that's not the time to be flippant about a person's great grief or anger about what is happening to him. His anger expresses a lot more than 'Why did God do an evil thing to me?' It's 'Why has my life turned out so badly?' And I'm not sure life turns out so badly. That's really what faith is. It turns out for good. I give thanks to God for having prostate cancer. I met all these wonderful people in the radiation suite and my life is enriched. When my prostate cancer returned during my sabbatical time, people said, 'Oh, I'm so sorry. Maybe you can make it up, take it another time.'

"I said, 'No, no, no. I got to know centering prayer and Thomas Keating. I'm better off.'

"The interesting part about this story is that the Episcopal Church tolerates ambiguity. We talk about Father God and Jesus Christ and Joseph and Mary, but I think Jesus was kind of bewildered by His life's mission. He represented a certain kind of entity; a certain kind of ethic in the universe that I really think makes a lot of sense. The Christness of us has to die and the Christness of us has to be resurrected again. We have to kind of sacrifice ourselves. *You* know that. When you and Karen came to the crossroads in your marriage, that was the sacrificial time of that relationship. It was time to fish or cut bait. Everything in the world that has that kind of meaning has that kind of death and resurrection. I'm expecting that to happen again. I see it all the time. I've picked up techniques over the years: helping these seniors in the Bronx with their SSI packages, with centering prayer or studying mindfulness with Jon Kabat-Zinn [a molecular biologist whose meditative method is designed to help people overcome stress, anxiety, pain, and illness]. Those are techniques. There are larger, powerful truths behind them."

Skip's deep belief along with his daily meditation and prayer are to me the essence of faith. He has not settled for easy dogma, nor has he felt that his faith is static. Instead, he does all he can to refresh and deepen it constantly, and he is unafraid of where his well-examined faith might take him or what it might demand of him, because "the God I know is a God of subtlety," he told me some years ago.

"God will never ask you to do something that will tire and deplete you and put you on the cross all the time. You don't have to do anything special. Just be in the moment."

My faith, however, did not evolve as did his. I held it easily when it was like a neatly wrapped package. Then the package tore and what was inside tumbled out and scattered like BBs and could not be gathered and rewrapped. I have yet to go beyond liturgy as Skip has. Where now the outward and visible sign described in the catechism to me reads, "Stop," he has traveled beyond it and found the inward and spiritual grace that eludes me. I marvel at the courage of his faith and his willingness to bare himself in it.

I still find myself at home in a church, but now it is more like revisiting the home in which I grew up. Apart from my membership on the Camp Stevens board, there are only a few signs of a connection to the Church in my life. Through Simon's and John's late teens, Karen and I maintained the practice that when we all ate together, one of us said the same short grace my father always offered. We each saw the illogic of this, though I like to think it was more hopeful and in honor of him than hypocritical. We also did it because we wanted our children to be aware that however ill-defined and unexpressed it might be, it's a good idea to think there is something bigger than us to thank. Even so, by the time our currently self-described agnostic sons were ready for college, we had abandoned the practice. But whatever their lack of belief, both Simon and John spent their junior high and high school years working Sunday afternoons at All Saints' to prepare for the feeding of the homeless on Mondays, and John became the assistant kitchen manager. For a couple of years, I had to travel often to London and always arrived on Sunday in time to attend the choral evensong in Westminster Abbey. While it did nothing to revive my faith, I love the service and the music. And although we all stopped attending Sunday services, even at Easter and Christmas, we kept going as a family on Thanksgiving, the one religious celebration Karen and I can give ourselves to without reservation because the service omits either creed and a lot of other dogma and concentrates instead on thankfulness. (She particularly loves the melodic hymns, whose theme is gratitude for the harvest.) I may not know whom to give thanks to or in what context, but I think it important to step outside oneself and acknowledge and be thankful— not just for the wonderful things in our lives but also for life itself and the hope to lead it well. After a couple of years of this, Carol Anderson began to tease me.

"I always know it's Thanksgiving when I see you in church," she said, each time with a laugh. She still does, but she has also spent hours talking with me about my struggle, constantly supportive, never proselytizing—as is true with Skip.

The one thing I *have* held on to is my father's message of love, and that has been my guide through life, with and without faith.

We all seek forgiveness for our various transgressions and betrayals. A beacon of Christianity is that sins are forgiven through faith, but as Skip shows, it is one thing to know you are forgiven and another to forgive yourself. My father is much on my mind at all times but has been even more so through the writing of this. I often wonder what he would make of what's become of my faith and whether he would be disappointed in me. I like to think he would hold me in his heart and prayers and hope the best for me, and that he would feel for me what he wrote to me all those years ago, that "the honest Atheist will find that God will probably say, 'You were mistaken, but come in.' " I imagine death and its aftermath are much on the mind of anyone in their mid-sixties; they certainly are on mine. I don't know whether I've found the right answer or ever will, but I like to think that the search itself is valuable. If I am wrong and my father was right about what happens after death, maybe I'll get to see him again. And maybe I'll finally learn the meaning of "God is no Kleenex."

An old joke: A river is predicted to overflow its banks and inundate the houses on the floodplain, so all residents are told to evacuate. One man, however, refuses to go. "God will provide," he says to the sheriff who comes to his home to offer a warning and a ride. The next day, when the water has risen to his porch, rescuers come by in a boat, but once more he refuses, saying again, "God will provide." The following day, the man has been driven to his roof by the flood. A helicopter comes, hovers over-head, and drops a rope ladder. Still he refuses, and yells as he waves it off, "God will provide!"

That night, he drowns and arrives in heaven. When God greets him, the man is furious.

"Why did you let me down?" he asks. "I trusted in you, and look what happened!"

"What are you talking about?" God replies. "I sent the sheriff. I sent a boat. I even sent a helicopter!"

Between my father and the multitude of priests and bishops I've been close to throughout my life, particularly Skip, I sometimes wonder whether, like that man, I've stubbornly ignored every opportunity to be brought back into the fold. All these people, whom I have liked and admired and in some cases loved, maintained their faith and grew in it. I do not repudiate their belief and think they are mistaken; I am now separate from their faith yet willing to believe that I may be mistaken. Not to do so would require that I devalue them, their ministries, their accomplishments, and the great good I have seen them do, and that is stupid on the face of it. They all found something profound and mysterious that transcends understanding and reason and that guides or guided their lives. Although it is one of the seven deadly sins, I envy them.

Faith's strength as well as its drawback is that it requires belief without proof. I don't think it's possible to understand God, but that doesn't mean much—I don't understand all of the natural world. I do know, though, that night follows day, and the seasons change. If I could have the faith in God that I have in these simple verities, I'd probably be better off. But these are congruent with laws of nature, while God is not a function of natural law, but of something greater and thus unquantifiable, unpredictable, and beyond reason—which is everything God should be. But for me at this point, it makes Him very hard to find. My faith as well.

I miss it.

ACKNOWLEDGMENTS

Friendship is more easily felt than described, but I know that without George Packard's presence in my life for nearly fifty years, I would be less. When we reunite, there is both ease with the past and openness with the present, as he has demonstrated in everything he's shared for this book. As college roommates, we were in faith, as he said at the time, "average guys skating around on the surface." In the years since, he has plumbed the depths. Skip and my father got on wonderfully, and I wish he could have seen Skip in his ministry. He would have admired the priest he is, as do I. This would be a far different book without Skip's contribution, and I am grateful to him. My thanks as well to his assistants, Terry Foster and Meghan Ritchie, for many kindnesses.

Among the dozen things one states belief in while reciting the Apostles' Creed is the Communion of Saints. Here's my communion of saints: my father and mother; Harold and Marie Robinson; Boone Sadler; Lauriston Livingstone Scaife; Anne Tumilty, now the rector of St. James Church in South Pasadena; Ivol Ira Curtis, the bishop of Olympia, whom I had known when he was in Los Angeles, and who offered to put

Acknowledgments

me through seminary and find me a parish in his diocese; Peter and Vicki Bergstrom, who, for forty years now, have continually made Camp Stevens better; and a long pewful of others I knew there. When I began this recollection, I hoped, after too many years out of touch, to reestablish contact with Andy Connolly, only to discover that two years earlier, while riding his motor scooter on Moen Island for the umpteen-thousandth time, he had pulled out to pass a truck on the now more crowded road, his white robe fluttering as ever, and another truck collided with him, killing him instantly. Also, my deep gratitude to Carol Anderson, who read these chapters in progress and offered thought-provoking conversation, as well as good companionship.

Dexter Fisher Cirillo and I grew up together (my father adored her). Her Peace Corps service influenced my decision to join, and her memories of those years and of my parents gave her a special perspective on this book, for which I give her, and her husband, Dennis Cirillo, affectionate thanks. The same to Bob and Sue Curtis, David James Fisher, and Edie Irons, longtime friends who read the manuscript and offered thoughtful and helpful suggestions.

I will forever be grateful to Vallerie and Gary Steenson, who answered a knock on their door at 7:00 a.m. one morning soon after they arrived on Fefan and came to my rescue, on that day and others. Thanks, too, to the Reverend Carl Gerdau, who spotted several potentially embarrassing errors; to Linda "Sherlock" Amster, who helped me track a Wolf; to Colleen Walker of the College of Emmanuel and Saint Chad; and to David Rogers, who would have preferred anonymity but graciously gave it up.

At Knopf, my thanks to Chip Kidd for yet another cover that instantly makes the heart of a book visible. Thanks, as well, to

Acknowledgments

Joey McGarvey, for continual assistance; to Kathleen Fridella, for shepherding the manuscript with great care; to Iris Weinstein, for another wonderful design; to Lisa Montebello, for seeing it through production; and, as ever, to Katherine Hourigan, who makes everything happen. Thanks as well to Carol Edwards, a splendid copy editor.

Jonathan Segal has been my editor and my dear friend for twenty-five years. Jon greeted with enthusiasm my proposal to write this book, as did Sonny Mehta. I am grateful to them, as I am grateful for, and admiring of, Jon's deft touch as an editor. I don't think anyone in publishing pays more or better attention to every detail or does it with more skill and dedication.

David Wolf unfailingly helps me make every book better. He spots incomplete thoughts and forbears complaint when the writing is slow. As does William Tyrer, who is always at the ready to read, comment, and help in every way. There are not adequate thanks for such friendship.

I wish my wife, Karen Sulzberger, and our sons, Simon and John, could have met my father, and I hope that this brings some of him to life. He and my mother were a constant source of love and support, which still carry me. My father preached a good sermon, but his actions, even more than his words, set the example I try to follow. I am lucky to have had him, and I know he would have been as proud of his grandsons as Karen and I are. Among the uncountable reasons I love Karen is that her keen sensibilities always help refine my thinking, and her partnership in all things makes life complete.

A NOTE ON SOURCES

I don't save a lot of e-mails, but for many years I saved almost
every letter I received. For the past forty, they have been in a
coconut husk–fiber suitcase-sized bag that I brought back from
Tsis. My mother, too, was a saver of letters (at least of mine),
and one day a few years before her death she presented me
with a grocery bag full of correspondence I had sent from college, Micronesia, and afterward, along with a binder of photos
interspersed with a narrative history of our family. Also, Jane
Kent Johnston kept a hundred or more letters from Truk,
which she returned to me decades ago, when we stopped dat-
ing but not being friends. This book would have much less
immediacy (and accuracy, memory being what it is, and what it
isn't) without these records.

I've also kept many college textbooks, among them the syl-
labi of Western Civilization I–IV, prepared by the teaching staff
of those marvelous courses that, alas, are no longer taught. I
would like to say that I drew my fast précis of them straight
from recollection, but I also relied on:

Hobart and William Smith Colleges
Syllabus of Western Civilization I (1962)

A Note on Sources

The Origins of Western Civilization
  Israel and Greece
  Prepared by the staff of Western Civilization I

Hobart and William Smith Colleges
Syllabus of Western Civilization II (1963)
  The Origins of Western Civilization
    Greece and Rome
  Prepared by the staff of Western Civilization II

Hobart and William Smith Colleges
Syllabus of Western Civilization III (1963)
  The Growth of Christian Civilization
  Prepared by Frank O'Laughlin and the staff of Western
    Civilization III

An affectionate round of applause to Mara Stearns O'Laughlin, who found the means to turn faded mimeographed pages into a set of paperback books, and so to preserve an ever-valuable education.

In addition to the primary texts of Saints Augustine, Anselm, and Aquinas, I also took guidance from *The Stanford Encyclopedia of Philosophy:* http://plato.stanford.edu/.

In describing Truk, I relied on letters I wrote to my parents and friends as well as a diary I kept, and I refreshed my mind with the first anthropological text on the people, Thomas Gladwin and Seymour B. Sarason's *Truk: Man in Paradise* (New York: Wenner-Gren Foundation for Anthropological Research, 1953).

For the timeline of events in 1968, I consulted *The New York Times* and http://timelines.ws/20thcent/1968.HTML.

Eric Lax's books include *Life and Death on 10 West,* an account of the UCLA bone-marrow-transplantation unit, and *Woody Allen: A Biography,* both *New York Times* Notable Books of the Year. *The Mold in Dr. Florey's Coat,* about the development of penicillin, was a *Los Angeles Times* Best Book of the Year. His work has been translated into eighteen languages.

A NOTE ON THE TYPE

The text of this book was set in a typeface named
Perpetua, designed by the British artist Eric Gill
(1882–1940) and cut by the Monotype Corporation
of London in 1928–30. Perpetua is a contemporary
letter of original design, without any direct historical
antecedents. The shapes of the roman letters basically
derive from stonecutting. The general effect of the
typeface in reading sizes is one of lightness and grace.

COMPOSED BY North Market Street Graphics,
Lancaster, Pennsylvania
PRINTED AND BOUND BY RR Donnelley,
Harrisonburg, Virginia
DESIGNED BY Iris Weinstein